Healing The Brain-Soul Connection

Don Stewart and Dr. Daniel Amen

Don Stewart Association
P.O. Box 2960
Phoenix, AZ 85062
www.donstewarttv.com

ISBN-978-0-9800760-0-4

Dedication

Dedicated to my family for loving me as a work in progress, looking beyond my faults, understanding my hunger for growth and truth so that I can give hope to more people on the road I travel that is always under construction.

My wife, Brenda, who has lived with a challenging ADD'er and still has heart – Brenda's heart.

My first-born, Renée, who was the brunt of a 20-year-old ADD father. She is a survivor...who has been able to do things that I would have never been able to do.

My oldest son, Kent, who, in many ways, has grown beyond my abilities.

My son, Brendon, who is anointed with bold faith for miracles.

My princess, Brenna, a leader that possesses the best of both her mother, Brenda, and me.

Acknowledgements

I would like to thank Debbie Martinez, who has been helping me for more than thirty years and can decipher an ADD writer's handwriting and for her editing assistance. Thank you to Lisa Godzich for assembling the various pieces and keeping us all organized. Also thanks go to Heather Cary for her research and assistance. Thanks to Colin Aldridge for his work on the cover art. Much appreciation goes to Bob Daniels for his trained eye helping with yet another book. Thanks to Dan Godzich for coordinating the project together with me and Dr. Amen from the start.

Rev. Don Stewart

Reverend Stewart and Dr. Amen have brought spiritual and medical healing together through *"Healing The Brain-Soul Connection"* – bringing hope, taking the stigma away from anxiety, depression and ADD. Don Stewart shows us how ADD can be a gift. A must read for anyone dealing with anxiety, depression or ADD.

- Sam A. Walters, N.M.D., founder of Wellsprings Clinic, using natural and traditional medicine.

Don Stewart's book is not like so many of the books we see today, a title which promises much, and has little substance. He included a Medical Doctor and Fellow of the American Psychiatric Association to aide with this project. This was meant to be a serious work to help millions of suffering people. I believe it has succeeded in bridging the gap between the mind and the spirit within each of us. Surely one cannot be successfully healed in soul with a mind that is not capable of focus or understanding. Or, what good is a sharp mind without a soul connection? This book is intended to give answers and those with a sharp mind and blessed soul will receive its answers.

- Dr. Ross Collette, Pastor, Deeper Life Ministries, Roseville, Michigan

"I can feel your heart in the words you've written and spoken in dialogues. I find that individuals with ADD, Depression or Anxiety often lack self-confidence. They view themselves as broken or as missing important parts. These insecurities keep them from reaching their goals because they don't feel deserving of having love, happiness and success in their lives. *"Healing The Brain-Soul Connection"* shows that these conditions are part of the "human condition" and part of what makes each individual unique. Your words help them to recognize their self-worth, learn to provide self-support, and acquire self-acceptance. These are the essential components of self-love which is the end result of *"Healing The Brain-Soul Connection."*

- Psychologist Ellen M. Diana, PhD, Phoenix, Arizona

The combination of Dr. Amen's pioneering work on the brain and Don Stewart's longstanding insights into the soul create this great work that is sure to increase the readers' understanding of their identity and their relationships to others.

- Dr. Leo Godzich, Chairman, NAME-National Association of Marriage Enhancement

This book is a great answer to prayer, a must-read for the guilt ridden, stigma-induced Christians who need a miracle for the mind but who have been too ashamed to ask for one. Finally someone had the courage to bring the church into the new millennium and specifically address issues such as depression and anxiety without condemnation. *"Healing The Brain-Soul Connection"* frees everyone suffering alone to get help, just as one with any other kind of disease would. As a criminal defense attorney for 13 years, I see so many young men who grew up in Christian homes who destroy their lives because society tells them it's better to destroy than to reach out and admit something is wrong. They don't think right, so they can't act right. Unfortunately it's not until many of them go to prison that they accept help. I'm proud of Reverend Stewart for writing a book that is truly inspired of God.

- Angela Collette, Attorney at Law and Member of LA Legal Productions, LLC

Don Stewart and Dr. Amen have tackled a subject that has been swept under the rug by most churches. This book will bring understanding and healing to those who suffer.

- Pastor Kerney Thomas Jr., Houston, Texas

TABLE OF CONTENTS

Vistana Resort

Just South of I-4/535 intersection

on 535

51047

ADJUSTMENT

DEPARTMENT ____________________

DATE ____________________

NAME ____________________ ROOM OR ACCT.NO. ____________________

DATE	SYMBOL	AMOUNT

DO NOT WRITE IN ABOVE SPACE

EXPLANATION		

SIGNED BY ____________________

Introduction

I have ADD. I don't consider it a weakness; I look at it as a gift. If you ask a doctor what ADD stands for, they will tell you "Attention Deficit Disorder," or they might tell you that it is really called AD/HD – "Attention Deficit/Hyperactivity Disorder," according to the DSM-IV.

First of all, I'll admit to you that I don't like the word "disorder." Nor do I consider that I have a disorder. So I call my ADD "Always Developing Destinies," or "Always Developing Hopeful Destinies."

I've often wondered, "Did God make me the way I am so He could use me the way He does? Or does God use me the way He does because I'm the way I am?" Whatever the case is, I'm grateful that He called me and gave me an assignment to Bring Hope and Healing to People. I suppose it is a two-edged sword. Maybe that is what the Apostle Paul meant when he said in Romans 7:21, "I find then a law, that, when I would do good, evil is present with me." What I call being spontaneous, Dr. Amen would call being impulsive.

God's grace is sufficient for me. Through the years, since I was a child, God has protected me. My life could have been a disaster, but for the grace of God. I have enjoyed 48 years of ministry. I have had the privilege of ministering in the palaces of presidents, prime ministers, and dictators. I have ministered to business people, educators and those involved in the arts. My greatest joy has been ministering to the common, ordinary people and to the poorest of the poor in 86 countries around the world. I've always been moved with compassion for people who are sick or in pain. The pain that moves me the most is emotional and mental pain. My slogan for years has been "God wants to heal you everywhere you hurt."

When I read Dr. Amen's books, *"Healing ADD," "Healing*

Anxiety and Depression," and *"Healing the Hardware of the Soul,"* I connected with what he had to say. I was fascinated with the idea that a person could see how their brain worked. I always knew that I thought different than most people. I didn't think inside the box. I saw things that others didn't see. Sometimes I would get an idea and share it with someone, and they would say, "That's crazy; that can't be done." There were times when I would get twenty different thoughts or ideas going through my mind at the same time. All of them, it seemed, were good ideas. Why was it so hard to do rote things that didn't excite me – things like fill out a questionnaire at a doctor's office, or study for a test? Why did I have such a hard time in school? I knew I wasn't dumb, but yet I felt stupid. I barely graduated from high school. I didn't really pass; I think they just wanted to get rid of a problem student. To me at that time, going to college was out of the question. I felt there was no way I could make it through college.

Thank God that in my early 20's I realized there was a difference between education and intelligence. I acquired a taste for knowledge. I intuitively knew I had to read things that I was highly interested in. The only way I could get through a book that had information that I needed but might not be interested in was to read three or four other books about something I was interested in at the same time. The books had to have a lot of self-interest – something I could hyper focus on. Sometimes I would start at the back of the book and read forward. I would jump from book to book when I would get bored. Most of the time, I would have to read a book several times before I was able to remember what I read. I am sure my retention level was very low.

At times I believe the Holy Spirit would bring things to my remembrance. I would be speaking and say things that I didn't remember studying or reading. I would say to myself, "where did that come from?"

I would go to a movie and really like it. Someone might say, "What was the name of the movie you saw?" I would say something like, "Uh…uh…I don't remember the name of it."

"Who starred in it?"

"Uh…uh…you know that actor that has black hair."

Things like that were common place in my life. Someone might say to me, "well that's what happens when you get old." I would kind of laugh and say to myself, "I must have been old all my life."

How many times did I lock myself out of my car – sometimes with the motor running? When they first started self-serve gas stations, you could fill up your car with gas, then go in and pay. I would forget and pull away without paying. Good thing that they knew me at the station. They would just call up one of my assistants and say, "He did it again, he pulled away without paying."

Just yesterday, I pulled into a gas station, put my credit card in, put the hose in the tank and then sat down in my car. As the gas was going in I heard the sound of the gas pump going, "click, click." I started thinking about this book and different ways it could help people. Then I started thinking about four other books I want to write. I started the engine, put the car in drive, put my foot on the gas pedal and pulled away from the gas pump. I started hearing the sound of the hose dragging behind the car. I put on the brake, looked out the rear view mirror – and there was the hose with the handle still in the gas tank – I had gone about 100 feet. "Oh no," I said to myself. A thought popped in my mind, "You better get out of here before someone sees what you did." Fortunately, through the years I have learned not to listen to those thoughts. I quickly said to myself, "You are responsible." So I took the hose to the cashier and told him what had happened. He came out and was able to fix it.

I choose to laugh at myself instead of beating myself up with thoughts like, "You're so stupid. What are people going to think about you?" Throughout my life there have been hundreds or even thousands of things like this that have happened to me – I'll save that for another book.

When I first met Dr. Amen and had my brain scanned it brought everything into focus for me. I began to understand why I am the way I am. I could see the over activity in my deep limbic system and the under activity in my prefrontal cortex. It was like a heavy load was lifted off me. There is an explanation for the way I am. My heart and lips were filled with praise to God. How good God is. How great God is. How grateful I was to God for "His mercy endureth forever." (Psalm 106:1)

If you or someone you love is dealing with ADD, this book will help you to understand both from a spiritual and medical viewpoint how to be the best "you" that you can be. Many successful and famous people have had the same challenges that you may have overcoming ADD and possibly dyslexia. You are in the company of such gifted people as Leonardo da Vinci, Emily Dickinson, Ralph Waldo Emerson, Robert Frost, Mozart, Picasso, Cole Porter, Frank Lloyd Wright, John Denver, Kirk Douglas, Dustin Hoffman, Anthony Hopkins, Steve McQueen, Elvis Presley, Jack Nicholson, Terry Bradshaw, Michael Jordan, Jason Kidd, Pete Rose, Thomas Edison, Will Smith…to name only a few. The list of those who have suffered with anxiety and depression goes on and on, from Ernest Hemingway to Abraham Lincoln.

To all my partners and friends, I can tell you this: Dr. Amen is not only writing to you from a scientific, medical point of view – he is a man of compassion who brings hope to people. He speaks from his heart. He has helped thousands of patients; his clinics have scanned over 40,000 brains. He has first-hand experience as a father of three ADD children, and has had to deal with anxiety in his own life.

I wrote some of the chapters, and Dr. Amen wrote some. A number of chapters are in an interview style, just as we recorded it. We chose to keep it in a conversational style. The chapters that Dr. Amen wrote will have his name at the head of the chapter and the ones I wrote will have my name. The ones we wrote together will have both names. In the chapters that are written in interview style (DS) stands for Don Stewart, and (DA) stands for Dr. Amen.

The chapters that I wrote come from my Biblical understanding and my own experiences, from both my personal life and 48 years of ministry. It is not my intention in this book to try to convert anyone to my particular doctrine, position, or belief. If I can bring understanding and help you or someone you love, I will have fulfilled my purpose for this book. To give you a point of reference, to help you understand where I am coming from, I will tell you I believe that Jesus Christ was born of the Virgin Mary, was crucified on a cross, was resurrected from the dead, ascended to the Father, and sent the Holy Spirit to be with us today. The Holy Spirit empowers people today with the Gifts of the Spirit according to 1 Corinthians chapter 12. The Gifts of the Spirit – the Word of Knowledge, Wisdom, Faith, Prophecy, Tongues and Interpretation, Discerning of Spirits, Gifts of Healing and the Working of Miracles – are still in operation today in the lives of certain yielded individuals. These Gifts can operate in many different ways through many different people. I believe that all healing comes from God – that Christ came "that they might have life, and that they might have it more abundantly." (John 10:10)

Dr. Amen is a neuropsychiatrist and child psychiatrist. He received his BA in Biology at a Bible School. I do not pretend to speak for him on the above position.

This book may be a first, where a TV Evangelist who believes in healing and miracles (that some would refer to as a faith healer), and a neuropsychiatrist have collaborated together to help people understand the connection between the brain and the soul.

I consider it a great honor to be collaborating on this book with Dr. Amen. There has not been one conflict with my faith or belief system with any of the scientific or medical information that he gives to us in this book. Or, as a matter of fact, in any of his books that I have read.

If you are dealing with anxiety, depression or ADD, there is hope for you. Take this journey with us and get understanding.

"Understanding is a wellspring of life unto him that hath it..." (Proverbs 16:22)

Chapter One

The Brain-Soul Connection

Rev. Don Stewart

Rev. Don Stewart is the host of the "Power & Mercy" TV program. For over forty years he has delivered the message of hope to millions of people in North America, Asia, Europe, Africa and South America. His Compassion Explosion meeting filled Madison Square Garden in New York City. He is known for his personal ability to minister to the humblest of people as well as Presidents and Kings. Rev. Don Stewart is the author of dozens of books including "How to Receive Your Healing."

Here Rev. Stewart explains his views on the Brain-Soul Connection:

> **Philippians 4:8 *"Finally, brethren, whatsoever things are true, whatsoever things are honest, whatsoever things are just, whatsoever things are pure, whatsoever things are lovely, whatsoever things are of good report; if there be any virtue, and if there be any praise, think on these things."***

As a young child, raised in church, I remember I used to get so confused on who I was supposed to pray to. Sometimes I would hear people pray to God, such as "Oh God, hear my prayer...." Some would pray to Jesus and call on His name, while others would sing and pray things like: "Come Holy Spirit, I need Thee." To my three year-old mind, I was confused. Should I pray to God...Jesus...the Holy Spirit? Who is God? What is God?

I had two older sisters and three older brothers. This was

about the same time that I couldn't quite comprehend the reason why my last name wasn't *Name*, instead of *Stewart*. With six of us, there was always a lot of teasing, bickering and outright fighting. My older siblings always knew how to get me started. They would ask me a question: "What is your name?" And my answer would always be – with a lot of passion – I would shout:

"My name is Donald Lee Name."

I can still hear it now, my brother Joe would say, "Well, you must not belong to our family because our name is Stewart." I can still see myself crying, running to mama, grabbing hold of her apron strings, clinging to her for reassurance. "Joe says that I don't belong to this family. I told him my name is Donald Lee Name." Somehow, my brain was not developed enough to understand the difference between saying Name and Stewart.

I just didn't understand. As I grew older and began reading the Bible, I began to realize how important understanding and wisdom is. ***"He that getteth wisdom loveth his own soul: he that keepeth understanding shall find good."*** **Proverbs 19:8**

I believe it's very important for one who is dealing with ADD, anxiety or depression to have an understanding of how the soul and the brain must work together to be healed. So let's start at the beginning. ***"And God said, Let us make man in our image, after our likeness... So God created man in his own image, in the image of God..."*** **Genesis 1:26, 27.**

1. **Who are you?**
2. **What are you?**
3. **What is your purpose?**

Our subject matter is who we are, not how long God took to make us, whether it was one 24-hour period, seven 24-hour days, or thousands and thousands of years, that is irrelevant to this subject. The Bible says **a day is as a thousand years, 2 Peter 3:8.**

What is relevant is, YOU are made in the image of God.

What is God? I believe that God is a Trinity: God the Father, God the Son, and God the Holy Spirit; Three in One.

***"In the beginning was the Word, and the Word was with God, and the Word was God."* John 1:1**

God is a Spirit. You are a spirit. Jesus took on the form of a body. You have a body. The Holy Spirit leads us, guides us, teaches us and helps us make good choices. This is what our soul does. It gives us a free will. That is what makes us different from the angels. We have a free will. It gives us the ability to choose.

You were made in the image of God.

There are three parts to you. You have a Body, a Soul, and a Spirit.

When we accept Jesus Christ into our lives, and are born again, old things are passed away and all things become new. God recreates our spirit. God is a Spirit and He lives in our spirit. This is where He abides. God is a Spirit and those who worship Him must worship Him "in spirit and in truth." John 4:23

In the Old Testament, the word ***soul*** comes from the Hebrew word ***nephesh***, meaning our being, self, passion, desires, emotions, thoughts. This is where we make choices. Personality. It's who we are inside, from the top of our head to the bottom of our feet. The Soul is felt and translated into active thoughts through the day-to-day function of the brain.

In the New Testament, the word ***soul*** comes from the Greek word ***psuche***, used in the same way as the Old Testament. The mind of man and the soul of man are used interchangeably in all the epistles written by the Apostle Paul.

The conclusion can be drawn that the soul and the mind are the same.

We get thoughts in our mind. We can embrace them or we can learn to reject them. **The soul is where choices are made.** It is our conscience.

We have a body. It gets sick sometimes. Is it because we don't take care of it? Is it because we are predisposed genetically to certain illnesses or diseases? Does a generational curse play a part in it? Do we not eat the right kind of food? Or because our food is so processed today, we don't get the right vitamins and minerals? Our body is the temple of God. We must be good stewards over it. God's plan for us is to ***"have life, and...have it more abundantly"*** **John 10:10** by using wisdom and understanding (Proverbs 19:8).

In **John 5:5**, Jesus came to a man who had been sick for 38 years. He had been trying to get into the water at the Pool of Bethesda. This was God's way of healing at that particular time. An angel would trouble the water and whoever got in the water first would be healed. He tried for 38 years and never made it. Can you image the pain he was in, not only physical, but emotional and mental disappointment? He must have felt like a loser. Someone always beat him to the water.

But then Jesus came by and asked a question: ***"Will you be made whole?"***

This book is about you being made whole in all areas of your life – body and soul. Your brain is a part of your body. Shakespeare said, ***"The brain is the soul's fragile dwelling place."*** Dr. Amen calls it the hardware of the soul.

How can your soul work properly so that you make right decisions if your brain is not working right?

Dr. Amen says, ***"A healthy soul actually enhances brain function and a healthy brain is essential to a healthy soul."***

Let's look at the hardware of the soul. Dr. Amen will now tell us about the brain.

Chapter Two

The Brain-Soul Connection

Dr. Amen

Daniel G. Amen, MD is a child and adult psychiatrist, brain imaging specialist, and a Distinguished Fellow of the American Psychiatric Association. Dr. Amen is the CEO and medical director of Amen Clinics, Inc. which have scanned over 40,000 brains. He is an Assistant Clinical Professor of Psychiatry and Human Behavior at the University of California, Irvine School of Medicine. He has appeared on the "Today Show," "48 Hours," the Discovery Channel, "The View," "Regis and Kelly" and HBO's show "America Undercover." Dr. Amen is the author of 22 books including the New York Times best-seller "Change Your Brain, Change Your Life."

Here he explains his view on the Brain-Soul Connection.

The word "soul" as translated from the Old Testament Hebrew means "all of your thoughts, feelings, personality characteristics, self, desires and passions." The soul is who we are inside from the top of our head to the bottom of our feet. The soul is felt and translated into action through the day-to-day function of the brain.

William Shakespeare said, "The brain is the soul's fragile dwelling place." We can now see actual evidence of this brain-soul connection through the latest brain-imaging techniques. These studies have so clearly taught me that when the brain is healthy, we are compassionate, thoughtful, loving, relaxed, and goal directed.

I've also learned that when the brain is sick or damaged we are unfeeling, impulsive, angry, tense, and unfocused, and it is very hard for our souls and our relationship with God to be at peace.

But what do I know about the soul? Isn't soul work off target for a scientist? Let me tell you about my own life.

I grew up in a very religious Roman Catholic Lebanese home with five sisters and a brother. I attended Catholic school until the end of ninth grade, and was an altar boy for many years. I was taught very clear ideas of right and wrong, good and evil, heaven and hell, and the judgment day. These beliefs followed me into adult life.

During the Vietnam War, I had a very low draft number and went into the US Army, where I trained to be a combat medic. I was fortunate enough to be sent to Germany instead of Vietnam.

In Germany, as a lonely soldier, I met Christine, a pretty, petite company clerk. She asked me to go to a church service with her.

It turned out to be an Assembly of God Pentecostal Church service. There was shouting, praying in tongues, and long, intense healing sessions. At first I felt strange, especially with all of the noise in church. As a Roman Catholic, I was used to church being a quiet place.

Not this church! There was a lot of intense emotional expression, but also a lot of fellowship and worship. I met a lot of wonderful people and became involved with Teen Challenge, a Christian group that worked with drug addicts. This was one of the factors leading to my interest in psychiatry. Many of the addicts had failed in traditional drug-treatment programs but were able to rid themselves of their addictions when they developed a deep faith and a connection with God. It was a fascinating process to watch.

After three years in Germany, I was discharged from the

military and attended Orange Coast University for a year and then Vanguard University, an Assembly of God Bible college in Southern California. I studied biology and the Bible. I wanted to be a doctor, but I also wanted a solid spiritual foundation for my life. Nothing in the Bible dissuaded me from medicine and nothing in my biological studies challenged my faith.

In 1978, I had the good fortune to be accepted to the charter class of Oral Roberts University (ORU) School of Medicine. Minister and faith healer Oral Roberts had worked hard to bring together spiritual healing and medical healing. I felt that this could be extremely powerful. I was suspicious that they accepted me because of my last name: The first graduate from their medical school would be Dr. "Amen."

ORU was an amazing place to attend medical school. We were taught solid medical science in an atmosphere of love, compassion and prayer. It was different from every other medical school in the country. We were taught how to pray with patients, take spiritual histories, and consider the "mind, body and spirit" in treating the whole person.

In a number of classes we struggled with the whole idea of sin and sickness. Many fundamentalist Christians believe that physical and emotional sickness came from a sick soul, and that you are more likely to be physically or emotionally sick if you have sin in your life. Others feel that we all get sick and die – it is part of the human condition. It only causes people to struggle with unnecessary guilt when you blame illnesses on sin. It was a sticky and complex issue.

After medical school I did my psychiatric internship and residency at Walter Reed Army Medical Center in Washington, DC, the military's largest hospital. As a resident, I taught a class to physicians and chaplains on the connection between medicine and spirituality.

I taught that 70 percent of the people in the United States

have strong religious beliefs. Health-care professionals, ministers and rabbis need to work together for the best interests of their patients. With each year of medical experience it became clear to me that there were many missing pieces to the puzzle of spirituality and healing.

During my residency I found that the more people were connected to their religious faith – no matter what it is – the healthier they seemed to be as a whole. They tended to need fewer psychiatric visits than those who were not connected to a body of believers.

This isn't just my observation. Researchers at Harvard, Duke and Johns Hopkins Universities have found that people with deep religious faith show greater physical and emotional health. Of course, one could argue that healthier people are more likely better equipped to make and keep connection with others and can thrive in groups of people.

The second piece of the puzzle became clearer to me while I was doing a fellowship in child and adolescent psychiatry at Tripler Army Medical Center in Honolulu, Hawaii. During this time I worked extensively with children, teenagers, and families. I consulted with schools, worked with medically ill kids, treated teens with severe problems and ran therapy groups for kids and parents.

I learned how important early development was to brain function. I saw how positive environments can enhance intellect and emotions. More often, I saw how negative environments can contribute to both psychiatric and learning disabilities. Any child psychiatrist knows that genetic vulnerability predisposes a person to problems, but the environment plays a large role in the expression of these problems.

The third major piece of the puzzle dropped into place in 1991. After military service I set up a private psychiatric clinic in California. I saw patients in both outpatient and hospital settings. I directed a hospital unit that treated drug and alcohol users who were also diagnosed with psychiatric conditions.

During one of the hospital's lectures I learned about SPECT imaging. SPECT stands for Single Photon Emission Computed Tomography. It is a technique that uses very small amounts of a radioactive compound to view the inner workings of the living brain. CAT (Computerized Axial Tomography) scans and MRI (Magnetic Resonance Imaging) look at the brain's anatomy, while SPECT scans help show how the brain functions.

SPECT was used to look at strokes, head trauma, and dementia. It was also being used by researchers to study depression, attention deficit disorder (ADD), schizophrenia, and obsessive compulsive disorder.

We could actually see brain patterns associated with "psychiatric" illness. That means that many mental illnesses were actually visible brain illnesses. As I learned more about SPECT and similar technologies, I believed they would change the face of psychiatry in my lifetime.

Since that time the Amen Clinics have spread to four different locations. Our clinics have scanned more that 40,000 brains. Finally, psychiatry does what other medical professionals do – we actually look at the organ we treat.

How does this relate to the soul? Does talking about the brain belong in church? Should ministers, priests, rabbis and other religious leaders learn about the brain? Is it sacrilegious to point to brain abnormalities as part of the reason people struggle with difficult behavior? I have been asked these questions many times by my deeply religious friends and colleagues. I was encouraged to stick to safer topics.

However, the connection between God and humanity, good and evil, and the brain is very easy for me. After all, I am a brain scientist, with a B.A. in biology from a Bible college. What could be more natural? What is unnatural to me is ignoring people with brain problems, even when they occur at church.

That's why I'm pleased to collaborate on this book with Rev. Don Stewart. My hope is that it will help lead people on the path to healing – healing of both the brain and the soul.

Chapter Three

My ADD Journey Through School

Rev. Don Stewart

"To put away aimlessness and weakness, and to begin to think with purpose, is to enter the ranks of those strong ones who only recognize failure as one of the pathways to attainment; who make all conditions serve them, and who think strongly, attempt fearlessly, and accomplish masterfully." – James Allen

The little chubby faced boy, only a month away from turning five, was sobbing and screaming, "No! I don't want to stay! Don't leave me here!" He held tight to his mama's leg as the teacher pulled him away. He cried "Don't leave me here." The teacher took him into the classroom, kicking and screaming. There was a little closet in the classroom; the teacher put him in it and locked the door. He kept screaming and crying, "Let me out! Let me out!" It seemed like an eternity had gone by until he fell limp on the floor, exhausted.

Finally the door opened and the kindergarten teacher said to him, "Are you ready to behave now?" This only ignited a new torrent of tears. As the teacher slowly closed the door again, he screamed, "Let me out of here!" His entire body was shaking and he slumped to the floor. He heard the click of the lock. Pounding on the wall, he cried "Let me out of here!"

How long did he sit there sobbing in the corner? "It must be night by now," he thought. When the door opened again he was still sobbing and gasping for air. The teacher took him out in the main classroom where 20 other children were. He wandered sheepishly over to a corner, not looking at the other kids. He let his mind take him out of the classroom. His thoughts jumped from one thing to another. It seemed to ease the pain he felt.

Then suddenly, he heard words that seemed to be coming from a distance, but were getting closer and closer. Then he recognized the words, "you stupid – you're a cry-baby. Donnie is a cry-baby. Donnie is a cry-baby." Over and over those words rang in his ears. He found himself kicking and throwing his fists, hitting anything or anybody that was in front of him. Finally the teacher came and took him to the closet again, and this time got a belt out, pulled his pants down and spanked him. He was so embarrassed because he didn't have any under shorts on. Those were a luxury his parents couldn't afford. He had five older siblings they had to feed. He really didn't feel the pain of the belt coming across his bottom. Surely it wasn't that hard; but he screamed as if he were being murdered. He felt a pain in his heart, an emotional pain that he would never forget.

It was hard for him to go to kindergarten every day; the only thing he looked forward to was nap time. He had to take a little blanket to school and every afternoon the kids would take a nap. During nap time he would daydream. However, one afternoon his daydreaming was interrupted by a very familiar feeling. He could feel his body tense up. He pressed his thighs and knees together. He tried to get the teacher's attention to see if he could go to the restroom; he knew he couldn't go without permission. He had gotten in trouble for this before. He rocked his body, held his thighs, but nothing seemed to help. It started with a trickle at first, and then all of it came. The blanket was wet. Nap time was over. He folded up the blanket hoping no one would notice, but his pants were wet. He pulled his shirt out hoping that the wetness could not be seen. Somehow he got by the rest of the afternoon without anyone saying anything.

Throughout his kindergarten school year, he tried to please everyone. The teacher was always saying to him, "You have to learn to listen to me." Why was he always thinking about something else? Even at this young age he knew there was something different about him.

He was so excited about going into the first grade. He didn't seem to be as shy and withdrawn as he was in kindergarten. He was curious and adventurous.

One day the teacher said, "We're going to show you a film today." He asked a kid next to him, "What's a film?" The kid snickered and said, "It's a movie, stupid."

"Oh no," he thought. "What am I going to do? Going to movies is a sin." In the Assembly of God Church that his parents took him to, he had heard the Pastor preach against going to movies and playing pool. But he was fascinated at the idea of seeing a movie and quickly dismissed the thought of sin.

Actually, it was a short black and white 16mm educational film. It had something to do with a manufacturing plant showing how their product was made. The lights were dimmed and the film began with flashing numbers in a circle, "6-5-4-3-2-1" – and then it started. He sat there totally fascinated. He had never seen a moving picture. He was able to stay totally still for the full 18 minutes. It must have been a record.

When the lights came on, the teacher asked, "Who can tell me about the film? What did you learn? What did you see?"

Up went his hand; he was jumping out of his chair with his hand shaking "I can! I can!"

The teacher pointed at him and said, "Tell us what you saw."

As he jumped up and down, he shouted, "Rain! I saw rain! It was raining!" Why was everyone laughing? The laughing seemed to build as it got louder and louder. What was so funny?

Why were they laughing? One voice stood out above the others "You're so stupid." Then he looked up and saw the teacher laughing. Slowly, he slumped back in his chair so far that you could barely see his head over the top of the desk. Tears began to run down his chubby cheeks. His face turned the color of an Arizona sunset. He was riddled with shame and embarrassment. He mumbled to himself, "I saw rain. I saw rain." This was 1945. It was an old black and white 16mm film with the grainy lines going up and down the screen. Then he said to himself, "I did see rain, but next time I won't tell anyone."

For the rest of the school year, he never volunteered to answer a question. He also never asked a question if he didn't understand something. He did a lot of daydreaming. He did try to please the teacher, but the seeds of him thinking that he was stupid were already planted.

The day after Labor Day in 1946 he entered into the second grade. On that first day the kids were waiting in the classroom to meet the teacher. When she came through the door, he gulped. She walked to the blackboard and wrote "Mrs. Stockton." He had never seen a woman that big. He was sure she was seven feet tall. (Actually she was probably about 6'2" and weighed about 270 pounds.)

She also wrote her rules on the blackboard. "A rule is a rule, you never get a warning. If you break a rule, you suffer the consequences," she announced. The first time you broke a rule, you had to go before the class, hold out the palms of your hands, and she would hit each palm three times with a ruler. The second time you would have to go to the Principal's office, where he would spank you with his strap. The boy told his father that this was unfair, but his father told him that every time he got a spanking at school, he would get another one when he got home. Needless to say, that happened a number of times.

One of Mrs. Stockton's rules was that you always went to the restroom before class. You would go whether you had to or not, because you would not be excused to go to the restroom during class. If you just had to go, you would suffer the consequences when you got back. First off, three whacks on the palm of each hand with a ruler. Second, spanking by the Principal.

Most of the time he would forget to go to the restroom during the break; but somehow he was able to make it through the class – except for one time. He had already broken one of her rules that day and had been whacked 6 times with a ruler. During the break he spent his time fooling around with other kids. When the bell rang he realized he needed to go – but it was too late; he knew he had made a mistake by not going to the restroom during the break. Then he started feeling the pressure in his bladder, and suddenly he had flashbacks to that day in kindergarten – lying on the blanket during nap time – he could feel his body tense up. Under his desk he squirmed as he pressed his thighs and knees together and started rocking back and forth. He looked up at the big clock on the wall and realized that he still had twenty minutes to go. He squirmed in his chair, crossing one leg over the other. Mrs. Stockton's voice came booming out, "SIT STILL." He slowly put his hands under the desk pressing them against his thigh, looking up every few seconds as he watched the second hand go by so slowly. He tried to let his mind wander and think about other things. Occasionally, he looked down at the reading book in front of him and tried to read about Dick & Jane. Moving his lips, he whispered, "Run, Spot. Run."

He felt a trickle down the side of his leg. "Oh God, please help me," he prayed. He looked down at the floor and saw a little puddle begin to form. Suddenly the bell rang, startling him. "What should I do?" he thought. "Maybe if I sit here no one will notice, and I won't have to hear those words again, 'Donnie is so stupid. He pee'd his pants.'" When everyone had finally left, he slowly got up and made his way out of the classroom; but there in the hall were six or seven boys, shouting, “Donnie is so stupid. He pee’d his pants.”

He hated school. He felt so many times like running away.

Somehow he made it to the sixth grade. By then he had become the class clown, making paper airplanes and throwing them across the room; mocking the teacher when his back was turned or giving him the finger, always getting a laugh from the other kids.

When he was 11 years old he got on a baseball team, but half the time he seemed confused because he couldn’t pay attention to the coach. (His coach was a man who really loved kids; his name was Jim Thornton.) He was very patient with him and tried to help him. Before their first game the players were warming up by playing catch. He wasn’t paying attention, distractedly looking around; when the ball his partner threw hit him in the nose. Blood went everywhere.

By the time he was a freshman in high school he was barely passing with D’s. His teachers were frustrated with him. “Donnie, if you would just try harder. You’re lazy. You just don’t apply yourself.” Mr. Ensign, the Principal, called him in the office several times, and said, “You are a smart kid, but you’re just not trying. We know what your I.Q. is and you should be making straight A’s, or at least A’s and B’s.” He thought Mr. Ensign was lying to him. He couldn’t be that smart. How could he be that smart when he was so stupid? But then again, he always got ideas that no one else ever thought of, just like the rain he saw on the film in the first grade. Yes, it was stupid, but it was something that no one else saw. Was it a gift? Was it a curse? What was it?

By the time he was 13, he began to see himself in front of people, a lot of people. At first he didn't know what he was doing. Was he a singer? An entertainer? He didn't know, he just knew that he was in front of a crowd. He was both visualizing it when he was awake as well as dreaming it when he was asleep.

It was September 1954 and, as a freshman, he went out for football. He had a good chance at making the team because it was a very small school. In fact, they played six-man football with other small schools in Arizona.

He was a chubby kid, not very athletic. As the players would take laps around the field, he was always last. His right knee was always in pain as he would lap around the field. One day the coach came to him and said, "Bugs," (he was nicknamed after the cartoon character, Bugs Bunny, after he was caught stealing carrots out of someone's garden.) "Bugs, you better go to the doctor and get checked out." The coach was a little short man named Rusty Winslow.

His parents took him to the only doctor in the little town of Clarksdale, Arizona. The doctor looked him over and said, "You'll be all right. You just have growing pains." But it hurt so bad that he had to stop playing football. His parents finally took him to the next town and had Dr. Brillhart look at him. The doctor told him to walk around the room. As he did, the doctor said, "I want to get x-rays of your hips. I don't believe the problem is in your knee." Well, he was right. Both of his hips had to have big steel pins put in with four operations. He walked on crutches for two years.

When he was in a classroom he loved being the center of attention. One time, as he was being his usual self – not paying attention in class, being the class clown and stirring up problems – he got caught throwing a paper airplane across the room. The teacher told him to go to the Principal's office. Donnie rebelled, and with an attitude that would try the most patient adult, he slowly got his crutches and started walking out of the room. He didn't use the door that was closest to him, but as slowly as he could, he made his way on his crutches up by the teacher's desk. All the kids watched this whole affair as he wasted nearly five minutes of class time. Frustrated, the teacher put a hand on his shoulder, gave him a little push and said, "Come on, let's speed it up." Donnie whirled around with his crutch under his shoulder and hand on the cross bar and hit the teacher as hard as he could right across the neck. With his crutch off balance and legs not holding him up, he hit the floor with a thud.

How long had he been there? Who were all the people around him? The nurse rubbed his head and said, "You are going to be all right. You are in the hospital."

He lay in the hospital for several weeks in traction with weights connected to his leg to stretch out and pull down his femur and hip so that they could operate on it. There was no orthopedic specialist in the little town of Cottonwood, Arizona. One would have to come from Phoenix to operate on him.

After suffering four operations and walking on crutches for two years, he was prayed for in a little Pentecostal church where he had a spiritual and physical experience. He threw his crutches away and began running around the church. He ended up at the altar, fell on his knees and began seeing the vision he had seen when he was younger. He saw himself in front of crowds of people. He knew he was not entertaining them, because he had a Bible in his hand. The scene kept flowing through his mind. Although he had never been more than 100 miles from home (the largest town he had been to was Prescott) he could see that the crowds flashing through his mind were of different nationalities – Latin American, African, Asian, Indian, and Scandinavian. It was like he was seeing a map of the world. Then he heard a voice – was it audible? Could anyone else hear it? Or was it something that he was hearing in his own mind? He didn't know; he didn't care. What he did know was that the message was for him. It said, "Take My healing power to the nations of the world."

After the powerful experience I had with God, I knew that I was called into the ministry. I found out about a Christian High School, a boarding school in Canyonville, Oregon, that taught the Bible. These days every major city has a Christian school, but back then there were very few with the exception of some Catholic schools.

It was going to cost $75 a month to go to Canyonville Bible Academy. That was a lot of money. My dad only made $400 a month – I guess I was fortunate because I was the baby of six children, and all my siblings were out of the home, making their own way. If they all lived at home and my parents had to feed all of them, there would have been no way. At the end of my sophomore year, my dad told me that if I worked all summer and would save $300, I could use $150 of it to buy my school clothes from Sears Roebuck, and the other $150 would go toward my tuition. He promised to come up with the other $525. He would only have to pay $75 a month.

Now I had something that I was really interested in. I didn't realize I could focus like I did. I hyper focused. I worked several jobs. I worked several hours a day as a soda jerk, and then at night I would work at the bowling alley, setting up pins. (No automatic pin setter in those days. You would sit on a ledge, and then after the ball hit the pins you would jump in the pit and set the pins up. You could actually work two lanes at a time.) I was paid 25 cents a game, so if there were four guys bowling and they bowled three games, that night I would make $3.00.

At a young age I was very entrepreneurial. I was always selling somebody something. One time I took some of my mother's squash out of the pantry and started selling it door to door. (In those days there were trucks going around selling fresh vegetables.) When I knocked on the first door, the lady came to the door and I asked, "Would you like to buy some fresh squash?" She looked them over and said, "How much are they?"

"20 cents."

"Oh son, go back to the truck and get me some more."

What was I going to do now? There was no truck.

That summer I sold Cloverine brand salve (this salve was good for anything), knife sharpeners, and a weekly newspaper called *Grit*. By the end of the summer I had saved $300. With $150 I was able to buy enough clothes for the school year. I was so happy; I was even able to buy some white under shorts. Going into my junior year of high school I wouldn't have to be so scared to get dressed after gym class.

To get to Canyonville Bible Academy, I rode a Greyhound bus that stopped at just about every little town between Arizona and Oregon. While on the long trip I mentally prepared myself for the worst. I just knew I wouldn't do well in school. I found myself getting D's and F's in this new school. I did get a C in Bible because I was able to memorize Scripture. I started hearing the same old storyline – "You're just not trying hard enough."

I was a little younger than most kids in my class; I was 15 and most of them were 16. I was also very immature, both emotionally and physically. My body did not develop as fast as my peers. Some of the boys were shaving already; but I didn't have any hair on hardly any part of my body. I suppose the hormones were a little late kicking in for me.

But about halfway through the school year I started to notice a beautiful brunette named Dorothy. She was the niece of a famous gospel music arranger and composer. She was about a year and a half older than me and very mature physically – and she thought I was cute. I think my hormones started kicking in about then. On the school campus there was an enclosed stairway leading up to the administrative offices. I was going up and she was coming down. She smiled at me and started kissing me. I didn't know quite what to do. I had never been kissed by a girl. She kind of led me through it. So we made out on the stairs of the administration building for a few minutes until we heard a door open up. We quickly straightened up and walked down the stairs; we didn't get caught.

Looking back, I can see that I was very impulsive. I also had a really bad temper. I always felt there had to be some kind of action going on. Late one afternoon I saw my friends standing over by a tree on campus, so I walked up to them. They were talking about climbing up the fire escape to the third floor of the girls' dorm – that was the floor that some of the girls we liked were on. I was especially attracted to a short little blond named Bobbie. The fire escape was like a single steel ladder attached to the wall of the building. One of my friends said, "Don, we dare you to go up there." That was all it took; I didn't stop to think of the consequences. I said, "Okay, let's go." Of course, they all waited at the bottom of the fire escape and I made my way up the wall to a window that opened into a hallway. I climbed in the window, talked about a minute with Bobbie, then climbed down the fire escape. When I got to the bottom my friends were all gone and there was the Dean of the school. He took me to his office and I was kicked out of school the next day. It is ironic that now, so many years later, I am serving as co-Chairman of the Board for Canyonville Bible Academy.

That was a very impulsive act. I just did it on a dare and didn't think of the consequences. Of course, probably all adolescents and teenagers are impulsive at times, but it's more intense and happens much more often with teenagers who have ADD. There are so many other incidents that took place as I was growing up; any one of them could have ruined my life. But there was a call on my life, and God led me to a man of God who discipled me and recognized the potential and the gift in me. I have been able to minister in so many different countries and cultures, that had I not been the way I am, I probably would not have been able to have done all that I have.

I have learned to build on my strengths and surround myself with people who are good at what I am not good at. If you have ADD or your child or a loved one does, understand that it's just a different way of thinking. There is help. When I was growing up no one knew anything about ADD; if you didn't do well in school, you were a bad kid that just needed to try harder. More and more people are being educated about the challenges of ADD. I always say, "It's not an excuse, it's an explanation." I quote from Edward M. Hallowell MD and John J Ratey MD in the book *"Delivered from Distraction:"*

"For thousands of years, teachers, parents, spouses, employers and just about everyone else missed the crucial point that paying attention is not always under voluntary control. Sometimes it is; if you ask people to pay attention, they can force themselves to do so for a few seconds. But after a few seconds, the mind's guard goes off duty, and the mind – impish sprite that it is – wanders off to wherever curiosity leads it."

I know that through the years I have confused people because at times I am distracted; it's not lazy attention. That's why I don't believe that Attention Deficit Disorder is a good description or name for this. There is no deficit of attention. If anything, it may be attention that is dynamic. It moves. It wanders. There are times that I hyper focus and shut everything out and have singleness of purpose. I used to think that I was not detailed or I didn't have a detailed mind. But that is not true. I can look at a report and if there is a little mistake, I will find it. If there is a misspelled word, I will find it (although I have a very hard time spelling myself.) I struggle with organization – my desk, my closet, my car. As a result, I surround myself with organized people (sometimes they drive me a little crazy).

If you have ADD, my advice to you is this: find your strengths and build on them. You will find that you are gifted. Develop systems around you to take care of your weaknesses. Get better at what you are naturally good at. Spend just enough time with your weaknesses to be able to function right. God has gifted us all in different ways. That's why we need each other. Don't dwell on the weaknesses; thank God for the strengths. Have understanding, choose your friends carefully and build on your strengths.

"...Let the weak say I am strong." Joel 3:10

Thank God for the gift of ADD!

Chapter Four

What Is A Neuropsychiatrist?

Interview Between Rev. Don Stewart (DS) & Dr. Daniel Amen (DA)

DS- Dr. Amen, you are described as a neuropsychiatrist. What does that mean?

DA- I think most people know what a psychiatrist is.

DS- Yes, and I've always been kind of leary of them.

DA- Me, too! Because, frankly, half of them are crazy! Psychiatrists take care of people who have emotional problems like depression, or problems with their thinking, like schizophrenia. A neuropsychiatrist is someone who also deals with the brain. Depression, ADD, anxiety disorders, manic-depressive illness, obsessive-compulsive disorders – are all disorders of the brain. I have a lot of extra training in the brain and how the brain relates to these disorders. What we do that is so unique in the Amen Clinics is we look at your brain because we think it's stupid to try to tell you what's the matter with your brain without looking at it.

DS- If I went to a typical psychiatrist, they would treat me without looking at my brain. Is this what you're saying?

DA- They would have no clue as to what's going on. The state of the art is 99% of psychiatrists make diagnoses exactly like they did in the 1840s. You know, Abraham Lincoln had problems with depression, and they made his diagnosis by listening to him talk. They described his symptoms and then they just watched him talk. So they did what we call "Mental Status Exam," and then they looked for symptom clusters. Now that we have the technology – and we've had it for fifteen years – we can actually look at the brain and see which parts are working too hard, and which parts aren't working hard enough, and then go about balancing your brain. Before we had this new technology, it was like throwing darts in the dark. Many people have gone to their family doctor, they've gone to their psychiatrist and told them their problem, they got medication, and the doctor had no clue as to what was going on inside their brain.

LOOKING AT THE BRAIN:

DS- That doesn't seem right to me.

DA- It would be like an orthopedic doctor setting a bone without looking at the x-ray, or a cardiologist working on your heart without an EKG or some sort of heart study. No other doctor or specialist in medicine treats their patients the way psychiatrists do. That's going to change. But it's slow, and we've been advocating for sixteen years now that you've got to look at the brain. How else would I know if perhaps you've had a brain injury and that is what is contributing to the problem? Or that you haven't had some sort of toxic exposure or brain infection? I don't know. How do I know unless I look?

DS- You know when I was growing up they used the word "crazy."

DA- Crazy doesn't really mean anything specifically. Most people are afraid of being labeled as crazy so they do not want to see a psychiatrist.

DS- I don't need some shrink messing with my head!

DA- Yes, that's exactly what they say. What you need is a great brain. And that's the thing that we do in our clinics. We want to optimize, improve and help you have the best brain possible. Because most people don't know that the brain is involved in everything you do. It's involved in how you think, it's involved in how you feel, it's involved in how you act, how you react, how well you get along with other people. It all has to do with the moment-by-moment functioning of your brain. There's no argument or controversy on this issue. Neuroscientists will all agree that your brain is the organ of behavior. But what blows people's minds is this simple concept that when your brain works right, when your brain is healthy, you work right. You act in healthy ways. When your brain doesn't work right, you have trouble in your life.

BRAIN SCANS – SPECT IMAGING:

DS- So, there are ways to actually change a brain that isn't working right and literally make a difference in someone's life. Is that what you're saying?

DA- Yes, and we can prove it. We scan the brain. We do a study called "SPECT." SPECT looks at blood flow and activity patterns, and looks at how the brain works. So, like we did with you, we scan you, see what's there, and intervene with supplements, medicine, whatever it takes to make your brain healthy. Then, we do a follow-up scan and ask, "How are you doing?" So, it's like plastic surgery. You can see the face before and you can see it after. That's what we do and we want to make your brain better! Why? Because with a better brain comes a better life!

DS- That brings up an interesting question. If, as you seem to imply, the human brain more or less controls a person's behavior, how does that affect the idea of a person's "free will"?

DA- You've probably talked a lot about free will in your preaching. Almost everyone has the idea that we all have the same level of free will. And it just isn't so. I wish it were. I grew up Catholic. I was a good Catholic...going to Mass every day...and believing that a person would go to hell if he's not good to his mother... the whole nine yards. Free will was a black or white concept.

So I started scanning people and I said, "Uh oh, we all don't have the same access to good brain health." What if you had a brain injury? Now you don't have 100% of free will. Maybe you have 50% of free will. So, I always say most of us have 85% of free will. But give you a six-pack of beer and now you have about 50% of free will. But what if you start with a brain injury from a car accident that was not your fault at all and you start with 50% of free will. Now, with that same six-pack of beer you might be left with only 10% of your free will, and maybe you kill somebody in an accident.

DS- Let's talk about that. As you know I believe in miracles and have seen God heal and deliver thousands of people, yet there are others who still need help. A lot of my friends believe that you can screw up the will power and you can do anything that you want to do. They've been able to accomplish a lot of things. I wonder if they walked in someone else's shoes and had to deal with what someone else had to deal with brain wise, would they still be able to screw up their will power and accomplish the things that they do?

DA- Probably not. It depends on the level of brain injuries they've had, the levels of toxicity they've had.

ALZHEIMER'S DISEASE:

DA- Let's talk about someone who has Alzheimer's disease. Most people know someone who has Alzheimer's disease. Are those people their "real" self, their "true" self? Would you say those people truly have access to 100% free will? Of course not! When you look at it on the scans, it's clear that it's a brain disorder or their brains are severely damaged.

HEAD INJURY FROM PLAYING SPORTS:

DS- What about a head injury?

DA- Let's take someone who has had a head injury, or played football in high school, had two concussions and been knocked out. We can see those injuries on scans. Do they have the same level of free will? No.

HEAD INJURY AND FAITH:

DS- You know a lot of people are so judgmental about this, even Christians.

DA- We're so quick, without the brain imaging, to judge people. If only they prayed more, if only they believed more, if only they tried harder they would do better. And when you look at it through the lens that I see now, it's just not true. We're lying. And the lies hurt people because when someone does something bad we tend to judge them. What we should actually do is evaluate them and treat them. And I think that's what Jesus would have done. He wouldn't have judged them and sent them away. He would say, "What's the matter with this person?" Then He would have healed them.

DS- So should we look at the brain just like any other organ in the body?

DA- Obviously the brain is sick and people don't think that the brain can have a problem like your heart can have a problem. If you have a heart attack, do you have sin in your life? Is that why you have a heart attack? No. But maybe it's because you had sin in your life, or you ate too much, you're overweight, you're smoking, whatever. But we don't have the same mindset with depression or with violence.

ADD AND DEPRESSION:

DS- Why is there such a stigma attached to depression?

DA- Because people don't see it as a medical problem. If you don't look at it, it's so easy to say, "Try harder." When I look at it and see the abnormalities in the brain, I see that the brain is on fire and working way too hard, or it's really low in activity. If you don't have that information, you will say, "Your character is the problem. You need to go to church more. You need to pray more." I am not opposed to church. I think a good church helps your brain work better. But too often Christians make a snap judgment and say, "I don't suffer like you do so obviously you're not trying very hard."

DS- You know, Jesus certainly dealt with that when He dealt with the little woman who was caught in adultery and said; "You without sin, throw the first stone." He was rough on those people who made judgments against other people.

DA- Well, He knew that there were no normal people. We hear people say, "I'm not crazy." But how many "normal" people do you know? I tell people that normal is a setting on a dryer, or a city in Illinois. We did this huge study looking for "normal" people. We screened 3,000 people who thought they were normal and by the time we got done with them, we only scanned 85 of them. And our criteria for "normal" was pretty simple: no psychiatric illness at any point in their life; no ADD, anxiety, depression, obsessive compulsive; no first degree relative with a psychiatric illness – mother, father, sibling, or child – because psychiatric illnesses run in families; no head injury, no significant substance abuse, and not taking any medicine. That's it! You'd think there would be a lot of people like that. Not that many! So, if you're suffering from a problem, if you're in pain, welcome to the rest of us! Be smart enough to get good help.

Chapter Five

Treating ADD And Losing Creativity

Interview Between Rev. Don Stewart (DS) & Dr. Daniel Amen (DA)

DS- Now, let me ask you this because even after I learned that I had ADD this is one of the things that I was a little reluctant to do. You know, I don't want something to take my creativity away from me. I was almost afraid that I would no longer be creative if I was treated for ADD. Because in my services, I feel that I am really led by the Spirit of God and I'm so spontaneous that I can feel people's needs and I'm able to flow in the Spirit and in the Gifts of the Spirit. That's just natural for me; whereas, the typical pastor would be a little uncomfortable ministering in that way. But, that's my thing, and I'm able to yield to God and help people. So, I'm sure there are other people who would have talents and abilities in creative areas that would almost be afraid to embrace this. You know, I have to tell you that in some ways I feel that ADD has been a gift from God to me.

DA- I think many people with ADD are highly gifted. And it's very common for ADD people to run big companies. Now, they're not the people that organize everything. If a CEO with ADD hires an ADD secretary he is more likely to go to jail because the IRS is going to get them. If you are smart, and that's one of the things that you are, and you surround yourself with people who organize you and organize your business, then you will be tremendously successful because some people with ADD have sixteen ideas in their head all at once.

DS- That's me. I get these creative ideas and really feel close to God because God is a Creator.

DA- Let me just say this about this thought of creativity, because you brought it up. We treat a lot of creative people and many of them are very worried at first. Artists, producers, and musicians ask, "What will happen to my creativity?" And it sort of depends. The answers are very interesting. Some get dramatically creative because they've been unable to finish things. We had one man who was a truck driver. He was an amazing artist but never finished his paintings. After he went on the treatment, he's now a world famous artist... because he finishes things. I treat a writer who takes her medicine when she's doing housework or dealing with her husband or her children, but will not take the medicine when she's writing because she actually likes having sixteen thoughts or plots running through her head all at once.

SUCCESSFUL PEOPLE AND ADD:

DS- Why do you think there are quite a few people who are successful that have ADD?

DA- Successful people have problems, it's just that they get help faster, so the problems don't ruin their work, or ruin their marriages, or ruin their relationships with their children.

RECOGNIZING ADD IN CHILDREN AND ADULTS:

DS- What would you say to a single mother who is living in the inner city, struggling to raise three children. The father is gone. She sees some behavioral problems in these children and she thinks that maybe it's because they're not going to church as much as they should, or maybe they're in with the wrong crowd,

which could all be true. How would this mother know if her son or daughter was dealing with ADD? What would be the signs?

DA- Well, you would look for a cluster of signs, over a long period of time. I say we all have ADD days, when we don't want to pay attention, or we don't want to get our work done, or where we have too many thoughts in our heads. But over time, do they have a short attention span for regular, routine, everyday things? One of the questions that I often ask my patients is, "How long does it take your child to do half an hour of homework?" I speak from experience because I have three ADD children. I know more about this than I want to know. For my son, a half an hour of homework would take him three hours to do with his mother yelling and screaming at him to sit down and get it done. If that's your life, then you need to start thinking about ADD.

SYMPTOMS OF ADD:

DS- What are some of the other symptoms?

DA- They also get distracted very easily. They see too much, they feel too much. Simple things like tags bother them or noises bother them. They have trouble sleeping and almost need the television on at night or some type of "white noise," like a fan going just in order for them to be able to concentrate. So, they get distracted easily.

ADD AND ORGANIZATION:

DA- They have problems with organization. Their rooms are not good, their book bags, their filing cabinets, their drawers are a mess. Organization is not their strength. Time is not their strength. They tend to be late. In fact, you know that someone is ADD at work if they're supposed to be there at 8:30 and they always show up at 8:37. What that means is that they don't actually get ready until something in their head says, "Oh my goodness, I'm late!" They need that stress in order to get them moving.

ADD AND PROCRASTINATION:

DS- Do they procrastinate a lot?

DA- They procrastinate – that's their middle name. They put things off, put things off, put things off until somebody's mad at them to get it done. If you're still procrastinating when you're a junior in college, you should have figured it out in high school that you need to get your term papers done early. If everything is done at the last minute, then you better think ADD.

ADD AND JUDGMENT:

DS- What about impulse control?

DA- Thinking before you say things, thinking before you do things. Is it helpful for you to say everything you think? Of course not! Relationships require tact, forethought, and some impulse control. But if you say everything that comes to your mind, you'll hurt people's feelings and then you could end up more socially isolated. So think before you speak or act. If impulse control or good judgment is lacking then think about ADD. Especially if clustered with those other symptoms.

ADD AND LEARNING DISABILITIES:

DS- How common are learning struggles or learning disabilities with ADD?

DA- They go hand in hand, almost like they're married to each other. About 60% of people with ADD have other learning disabilities. Reading problems and writing problems are all associated with ADD. My son had a handwriting problem. If you asked him a question, he could tell you the answer. If you asked him to write it, he would stare at the paper for two hours and come out of his room with two sentences on a question as broad as "What did you do over the summer?" But if you asked him to verbalize it, he would be able to tell you with no problem.

DS- I do a lot of writing. I do a lot of writing to my partners and I still like to write with a pad and pencil instead of using a computer. I can type, but I seem to get more inspiration going when I write by hand. I will sit there and it seems that God is just pouring revelations into me and I will get going so fast that I can't read my own handwriting when I finish. Thank God, there's one girl who works for me and she's probably the most important person that works in that office. She can actually read my handwriting.

ADD AND HANDWRITING:

DA-That's another symptom. Bad handwriting or poor handwriting is very common in people with ADD. In fact, many ADD adults print rather than write in cursive because nobody can read it.

DS- That's interesting because I half write and half print. I print some and then I guess I get bored and have to switch; or, I can't spell and just draw a line to cover up the fact that I can't spell. Actually, I used that technique in high school. When I couldn't spell something, I would scribble it so the teacher wouldn't notice that I couldn't spell the word.

DA- One of the common accommodations that are made for kids with ADD is to get them programs like "Drag and Dictate." This allows them to speak and the computer will type it for them. Some of the kids we do that with go from getting D's and F's to all A's and B's because it was just a writing disability that was the problem.

DS- Now some kids I've noticed have a hard time if they're trying to copy something from the blackboard onto paper. What's going on there?

DA- Well, they get distracted so they forget by the time their brain gets to the paper because they had four other thoughts in between.

Chapter Six

ADD And The Prison Population

Interview Between Rev. Don Stewart (DS)
& Dr. Daniel Amen (DA)

DS- What about the prison population? I have a brother who has spent time in prison and obviously he had some issues. I'm sure he has ADD as well. Our prisons are filled with people who have ADD. Do you know what the percentage is?

DA- One study was 75%, but I think that number is too high in general. It's probably closer to 20% to 40% of people in prison would meet the diagnostic criteria for ADD. And if you don't treat it, when they get out, they're likely to come back to prison.

DS- I've been thinking about all the things you have been saying and you can tell I have ADD because now I'm off topic and my thoughts are going in different directions, I call it chasing rabbits! This is such an interesting thing to me; when I went to your clinic and I had my brain scanned it was a fascinating experience. It was an interesting scan.

DA- It was a very interesting scan.

DS- One of your doctors brought you a copy of my scan and you looked it over, right? One of the things that helped me when your doctor pointed out to me, the ADD part is where I had what looked like little holes in my Frontal Lobes.

DA- Decreased Activity. In the front part of your brain that got worse when you concentrated.

DS- Right. That was like the old saying, "A picture is worth a thousand words." That picture helped me to understand that after all these years, there's a reason. As I told you earlier, I really feel that ADD has been God's gift in my life, in spite of its polarity. It's like the Apostle Paul said: *"Every time I do good, evil is present."* You know, what is meant from that Scripture reference? God turns it into something good; He reverses the curse! So the ADD that I have genetically, do you think I might have inherited it from my parents?

DA- What do you mean? That you might have inherited it? You talked about your brother and you said he got into some trouble and was in jail.

DS- I think it started with my Dad. I didn't find out about this until many years later but I always knew there was something different. Of course, that generation of men were not very affectionate. He was very, very distant. I was one of six children. I came from a very poor environment. I was brought home to a little room with a dirt floor and a canvas top with five older brothers and sisters. When my Mom was carrying me, my Dad took off and left for Michigan because he was already married to two other women at the same time. I have acquired some letters recently that he wrote during this whole time. He used expressions such as, "Something was driving me, like a dark force and, I don't know why I have such dissatisfaction." He left his first wife when he was 25 and had 2 children. He took off and deserted her. He just disappeared.

DA- Impulsivity.

DS- Yes.

DA- Not thinking about the consequences.

DS- Then he went to California and married another woman. Took off on her, didn't get divorced. Ended up with my mother, and she didn't go anywhere with him but to church. She was a really dedicated Christian. There he had an "experience." He changed his life. You could see that he had a gambling problem.

DA- That's common with ADD.

DS- He had an alcohol problem. He used to do those things and then just like that, he changed. He started hearing preaching from a very strong Pentecostal preacher who convinced him that he needed to go back to his first wife because of the way they interpreted Scripture. But he was still married to his first and second wife and decided to leave these six kids and go back to his first wife and live with her. You could see the torment in his letters that he wrote. He was totally tormented this whole time. I thought he was impulsive and just acted on things. But, thank God, he was able to change his life. By the time I came along, he was older, he was a man that read his Bible every day, and he became a very solid citizen. There was a drastic change in his life. This was a total act of Grace – and showed how God can turn a life around.

DA- As you know I grew up very Catholic. When I was 18 I went into the military and I ended up in Germany where I met a really cute company clerk. And when I asked her out, she said, "Would you take me to church?" "Church?" I said. She said, "Church." She took me to a Pentecostal Assemblies of God healing service at the 97th General Hospital in Frankfurt, Germany, which just scared the socks off of me! Because, here are these people who are shouting and praying in tongues. Where I went to church the Nuns always said that God was a little bit irritable and you needed to be quiet in church. These people were not quiet! I tell you that to tell you that I got involved with Teen Challenge, which is a Christian group that deals with drug addicts. Years later I figured out why I think they are one of the most effective treatment programs for drug addicts on the planet. Why does that work? Why does having a religious conversion and developing a strong religious belief turn someone's life around from things like heroin, cocaine, and methamphetamine? I think it's three things:

1. The first thing they do is give you a family. When you're welcomed into a church, into a body of believers, you have a family and often your real family has turned their back on you because they're tired of your stuff.

2. The second thing they do is give you a set of rules. It's called the New Testament. We live our life this way.

3. The third thing is, and a lot of my religious friends don't like to hear this, they give you a lot of fear; they give you a lot of anxiety.

A lot of people with ADD don't have enough anxiety. That's why they can ride motorcycles crazy down the highway, or they can jump out of airplanes, or they can rob the grocery store without thinking about the consequences.

DS- What do you mean not enough anxiety?

DA-You see, if I get the thought that I'm going to rob the grocery store, immediately my brain starts saying, "No you're not. What's the matter with you; are you stupid? You could get caught and you don't like institutional food." I mean the anxiety kicks in and prevents me from doing bad things. When I got involved with the Assemblies of God, I learned about the "Rapture" – Jesus is coming, and He's coming tomorrow or maybe today – are you ready? If you're not, you're going to be left behind! So, all of a sudden, there was anxiety, and Catholics have plenty of anxiety over burning in hell. And if you're not quite good enough, you're going to purgatory. But all of a sudden, the anxiety level is raised and there are consequences, Eternal consequences for your behavior, and I think that's helpful for a lot of people with ADD because they don't have enough anxiety naturally. We all need some anxiety. If you don't have any anxiety, and you don't pay your taxes, you'll end up in jail. If you don't have anxiety and you meet a beautiful woman at the bar you'll say, "I'll go and take her home with me," before you really know her. What I have to say about that is, don't you remember the movie, *"Fatal Attraction"*? Right? Before you let somebody know where you live, you should probably get to know them a little bit. But anxiety often helps people with ADD.

CHAPTER SEVEN

Depression

Interview Between Rev. Don Stewart (DS) & Dr. Daniel Amen (DA)

DS- Now let's talk about depression a little bit more. Is this one of the most diagnosed psychiatric illnesses that there is?

DA- Okay. We've been talking about the three most common psychiatric illnesses – ADD, anxiety and depression. Of the three, anxiety is actually the most common. People suffer with anxiety disorders more than anything else worldwide. Next is depression. Besides having a baby, depression is actually the number one reason women are hospitalized between the ages of 18 to 44. It is the number one medical reason for hospitalization. It's very common. Suicide is the eighth leading cause of death. Depression is very important because it's a medical illness. Just like you have diabetes, you have depression; so is having heart disease or cancer; so is depression. Left untreated, depression is potentially lethal.

DS- Can you have different degrees of depression? For instance, can you have low-grade depression where you think, "Everyone's like this" or "Everyone feels this way." Where you get up in the morning and just have to pick yourself up by your bootstraps. Every morning you have to get up and make yourself get going and you start thinking after a while that it's just a common thing.

DA- There's this thing called "Dysthymia." Dysthymia is a chronic low-grade depression over a long period of time. It's very hard to be married to these people because they are so negative. They're not fun. They don't like to joke around with you and they're not playful. So, getting that treated can be very helpful, especially for the people you love. Depression is a spectrum from people with a mild sadness, who maybe are only sad three days a month, and there are other people who are so sad and in so much pain that they want to die.

DS- Well, how can you tell if you're just having a blue time in your life? This is so hard because everybody has good days and bad days. Is it more prolonged? Is it more intense?

DA- When you think about it, if it lasts for more than a couple of weeks you need to think about a medical depression or a clinical depression. All of us, if we lose our partner or if we lose our parent, we're going to go through a period of grief and mourning. But when it gets prolonged, when it gets to be more than a couple of months, then you need to start getting worried and thinking about getting the right help for this person.

DS- So, can depression come on without some big trigger or without some crisis? Can it come on unexpectedly?

DA- I often think of three causes of depression:

1. Biological causes and physical causes of depression.

   If you have a head injury, you're more likely to get depressed. If you have a stroke, especially to the left front side of the brain, which is the happy side of the brain, you're more likely to become depressed. Certain types of medication: blood pressure medication, or heart or pain medications, can make you depressed. If you have some vitamin deficiencies, if you're lacking Vitamin D, which comes from the sun, which can lead to depression. So there are biological causes that cause depression. If you drink too much alcohol, it can make you depressed. That's a biological cause of depression because alcohol is a downer to how your brain works.

2. There are psychological causes of depression.

You think negatively. You say you're a pessimist, because then you won't be disappointed. Well, you're also more likely to kill yourself because you will be more likely to suffer from depression.

3. There are social causes of depression.

You lose your job or you have a financial crisis. Someone you love dearly leaves you or they die. The people who have the biggest struggle with depression are the ones who get all three of those things at once. They have a biological vulnerability – maybe depression runs in their family. They have a tendency to be negative thinkers, and then they lose their job. So it tends to be all those things that come together at one point that makes people feel really hopeless.

Chapter Eight

Post Traumatic Stress Disorder

Interview Between Rev. Don Stewart (DS)
& Dr. Daniel Amen (DA)

DS- You know, I've dealt with a number of people that have asked me to pray for them for Post Traumatic Stress Disorder. I've often wondered about them. Say for instance people coming home from war. Two guys go to fight in a war. They go through exactly the same things and one seems to suffer from Post Traumatic Stress Disorder while the other seems to adjust just fine, or two girls have been raped while as a teenager. One seems to be able to adjust better than the other one.

DA- You have to think about the brain. What were their brains like before they went? I was an Army doctor for seven years. I actually wrote an award winning paper on "Post Vietnam Stress Disorder." The point of the paper was that it depends on the brain you bring into the war as opposed to the brain you bring home after the war. So, you're right. The exact same traumatic situation of seeing your buddy's head blown off or leg blown off – one person will come home and never be able to forget about it and the other one will come home and be sad about it but it won't ruin their life.

What are the factors in the things that we bring to a traumatic situation? What are your genes? Do you have people in your family that have tendencies towards depression? Then you're more likely to be depressed; that's a vulnerability. Did your mom smoke when she was pregnant with you? That's a huge vulnerability to what we find. Don't smoke when you're pregnant! It's very bad for babies. Have you had any head injuries? Have you used drugs? So, I think that the brain has a certain level of resilience or reserve. And you have 100% reserve when you're born. If you played football in high school and you had four concussions, now you only have 50% reserve. And if you were drinking a lot, you now only have 30% reserve. So now when you go to war and you see these traumatic attacks, it takes away the rest of your reserve.

But, let's say your mom took care of herself when she was pregnant with you and didn't smoke, you didn't play football, you played tennis, you weren't in any bad car accidents, you didn't do drugs because you thought they were stupid. When you see that same traumatic event, you have 100% reserve and it takes some of your reserve away, but it doesn't ruin or dominate your life.

DS- Now when you take a scan, does Post Traumatic Stress show up in a certain way?

DA- Yes. Actually we see patterns on the scan. It's called our "Diamond Pattern." The emotional brain works too hard. They tend to be obsessed, depressed, anxious, and they can't let go. Through some psychological treatments we seem to be able to calm down that part of the brain.

DEPRESSION AND SUICIDE:

DS- Dr. Amen, we get so many prayer requests from people who are suffering from depression and really, it breaks my heart with the amount of letters we get about suicide. Let me share a couple of letters with you:

> ***"Recently I have thoughts racing through my mind about killing myself. To let you know, it is 1:00 am***

> ***in the morning and for three months, I have been going through this dark, gloomy place in my life. Tell me what to do."***

DA- Well, the fact that the writer is reaching out is a good thing. But the fact that he's been like that for three months means that he is probably very depressed. With those kinds of thoughts, don't drink, because it might dis-inhibit him and he might kill himself. Get professional help. It's at that point that seeing well-trained specialists can make a huge difference in your life. I see that happen in our clinic every day.

DS- Here's another letter I want to share with you:

> ***"I feel like I am living in hell. I feel the need to take my own life and end this pain."***

These people are suffering. I have a lot of people writing to me and say they are in similar situations and God touched them. This one's grandson has Touerette's Syndrome and he is depressed. The family needs help; it seems to be tearing the family apart.

TOUERETTE'S SYNDROME AND DEPRESSION:

DA- Touerette's Syndrome is very interesting. It's a "tic" disorder where people have both motor tics; physical tics like blinking of the eyes, or jerking of the head; and there are vocal tics where they make noises – coughing, puffing, blowing, barking, and sometimes even swearing. Very commonly associated with ADD. Also with Obsessive Compulsive Disorder and depression. Many people with Touerette's need really good psychiatric help and without it, they can get depressed and sometimes even suicidal depressed. It is estimated that 55% of the population has at some time in their life had suicidal thoughts. Just because you have them, don't let it freak you out, because it doesn't mean you are mentally ill. But, if you have them and they are not going away, then it's usually a sign of depression and getting help is critical. Suicide is the eighth leading cause of death and you don't want to do that. What I tell my patients is, "Suicide is a permanent solution for a temporary problem or feeling." Suicidal thoughts go away, but if you kill yourself, then that's it. It's the end of the ball game.

DEPRESSION AND SUICIDE:

DS- If a person has attempted suicide, is it more likely that they'll attempt it again?

DA- More likely, yes. Other people say they are doing it for attention. Maybe, but they're also more likely to kill themselves. I actually have done a lot of research on suicide. The people who actually kill themselves have a very different brain. And getting it properly treated either with medicine, supplements, or exercise can make a tremendous difference. I know the pain of suicide. When my son, who I adopted, was 9 years old, his biological father shot and killed himself. To see the pain in his eyes was just awful. My son-in-law's father killed himself and you can still see the fallout of it. I tell my patients, if you kill yourself, you've just given your child a 500% increased chance of them committing suicide. We're connected as families, so don't do it.

DS- Let me read part of an email I received:

> ***"I feel like I am beautiful and I have a lot to offer, but I just can't stop feeling depressed. I need help."***

What do we tell these people?

DEPRESSION AS A MEDICAL ILLNESS:

DA- We tell them that depression is real. It's a medical illness. Just like your arm can have problems, your brain can have problems. If it doesn't go away, there's still hope.

DS- So, then, it's no different than any other part of our body?

DA- Your brain is an organ just like your heart is an organ. Your liver is an organ like your pancreas or your stomach or your gallbladder.

Chapter Nine

Depression And The Church

Interview Between Rev. Don Stewart (DS) & Dr. Daniel Amen (DA)

DS- I think there is a lack of understanding in many churches. There are people who go to church and if they are taken to the hospital because they have a kidney stone, then the entire church will pray for them. But if they had to go to the hospital because they were so depressed that they felt like they were going to take their life, they probably wouldn't tell anybody.

DA- No, but the church should pray for them. And they should get support for it. But because we don't understand it unless we've suffered from it, we tell people, "Snap out of it!" You can't tell someone with a heart arrhythmia to just, "Snap out of it!" How stupid does that sound? It's the same thing with depression or panic attacks.

DS- I believe that's an indictment of the church. I think the church is in a sad state when people who are suffering don't feel comfortable enough to get the help they need at church.

DA- I think I told you that I went to Oral Robert's University. I went to Medical School there and had a wonderful Christian environment. There were a lot of people at ORU that thought if you were depressed then you had sin in your life. I thought, "Does that mean that everyone that dies of heart disease has sin in their life?" Come on! It just doesn't make any sense to have that attitude.

DS- Here's another letter:

> ***"I am married to a beautiful woman. We have a beautiful baby girl, but I came close to killing both of them last night."***

This man needs help!

HEAD INJURY AND VIOLENCE:

DS- What about domestic violence?

DA- What we've found is, because we do a lot of work with murderers and domestic violence, he may have had a head injury. He may have a serious mood disorder. When you get to the underlying cause and treat it, you literally can change someone's life.

MISDIAGNOSING:

DA- Too often you go to a psychiatrist or the family doctor, they give you Prozac or whatever and they never look at what they do. I have this one fascinating case. This woman had depression and she was a pastor's wife and was put on Prozac and she felt a lot better. A driver came up next to her in a truck. He looked at her, and she opened her blouse to him. Something she had never done in her whole life! What we see, if it's not the right medicine for you, it can actually dis-inhibit you and make you worse. The imaging helps us to target treatment. We don't prescribe medication without targeting the treatment to the brain.

DS- You hear these horror stories of how people somehow went on Prozac, or another anti-depressant, and it made them suicidal or they go crazy. Then other people say "it saved my life."

DA- It happens. If you never look at the brain and just treat people based on symptoms, you're going to make mistakes. That's one of the reasons why I like doing imaging. Before I did imaging, I was just a psychiatrist for nearly 10 years and I hated it when I would make a mistake like that. Now that I look at the brain, I make fewer mistakes like that.

DEPRESSION AND PROZAC:

DA- Depression is not just one thing. We've been talking about it like it's one thing but it's not. What we've seen is that it's actually seven different things. Sometimes you have depression because your brain works too hard and you can't stop thinking. Sometimes you're depressed because your brain doesn't work hard enough...you just can't cognitively get your thoughts together.

The person whose brain is working too hard, if you give them Prozac it calms them down, they feel better, they're not obsessed anymore. The person whose brain starts low in activity, give them Prozac and it calms it down, makes it even lower in activity, so now they do more stupid, impulsive things. You need to target the treatment to your brain. You can't just say, "I'm depressed; I'll take Prozac." That approach is not a good approach!

DS- So, drugs like Prozac, when taken by the right people, are like a miracle.

DA- Yes, like a miracle.

DS- For the wrong people, it can be devastating.

DA- It can be a disaster. I've written several books. One is,

"Healing Anxiety and Depression." It talks about seven different types and if you have this type, there's a checklist in the book to help people to think about this medicine, or don't think about that one.

DS- So that's why it's so important from a physician's standpoint for you to be able to look at the brain.

DA- Otherwise, how do I know what is the proper treatment if I don't look?

DS- To help you decide what type of medicine is the right kind of medicine for that person?

DA- Right, and if people can't find a doctor like us, they can pick up one of my books and get a lot of helpful information out if it. It will help them decide which symptom they have that could be the problem with their brain, and help them decide which action to try first. I think that when you go to the doctor, you should be educated. If someone's going to be messing with your brain, you want to know a lot about it!

DS- We really need to take charge of our own health, don't we?

DA- Absolutely!

DS- So many people are intimidated by doctors in general. For years, if I go get my cholesterol checked I want a copy of it because I take charge. I want to know. It surprises me sometimes how dumb some doctors can be. I know that's a wild statement!

For instance: I've read a lot of books and a lot of psychiatrists didn't make sense to me until I read some of your writings. The thing that stood out to me the most was when you said we are the only medical profession that tries to treat something

without looking at it. That just clicked inside of me and made so much sense. I certainly wouldn't want someone to fix a broken arm without taking an x-ray first.

DA- When we don't look, that causes us to make mistakes, and I don't like that. I like it when my patients get better. I don't like it when they get worse.

DS- So we have to take charge of our own health and educate ourselves. I've written a book called, "Don't Worry Be Happy" and another one called, "*How To Receive Your Healing.*" People can go to our web site www.donstewarttv.com and get valuable information on resources that will help them, including your books, CD's and DVD's to educate themselves. It certainly has helped me.

Let me share one more letter that I received from a young lady and then we'll move on:

> ***"I'm trying so hard to see the reason why I'm on this earth. The other night, as I sat in my room and thought about my life and where my life has gone and come, I'm a wasted life of God and I have no reason to be here on earth. About three nights ago I was sitting on my bed late at night and I prayed to God, tears began to pour down my face. I asked God for forgiveness that I was not a good enough soul to be living on this earth."***

You can see there's evidently a lot of guilt and a lot of things going on in her mind to make her believe she's not good enough. Is that a common thing?

CHAPTER TEN

Depression And Distorted Thinking

Interview Between Rev. Don Stewart (DS) & Dr. Daniel Amen (DA)

DA- It's depression. But it's also distorted thinking. That's a huge **ANT**! That's an acronym I use for **AUTOMATIC NEGATIVE THOUGHTS**. It's clear this woman is living with a lot of Automatic Negative Thoughts. Whenever you feel sad and you get a suicidal thought like, "There's no good reason for me to be living," ask yourself one question: "Is it true? Is that thought really true?" Can you absolutely with 100% certainty know if that thought is true? And usually the answer is "NO." We can't know the mind of God. You may be going through this so you'll have empathy. I've often wondered why did I end up having three kids with ADD? So I can understand people with ADD. There are times in my life where I've gone through grief or depression. It makes me a better doctor because now I can understand what other people that I'm helping are suffering with or dealing with. So when you get these negative thoughts, challenge them, question them, and don't just believe them. We should have taught this in third grade because third graders are filled with **ANTS**.

DS- So with ADD you talked about depression, that there's seven types of depression. You stated that there are six different types of ADD.

DA- That's right. There are six different types, so, don't give everyone Ritalin. For the right person, Ritalin is a miracle. For the wrong person, it's a nightmare! I have one patient who is the son of a pitcher for the Cleveland Indians. By the way, this pitcher has given me permission to talk about his family. Well, the son had all the symptoms of ADD and was put on Ritalin and quit sleeping. The son became anxious, angry, and suicidal. The father said, "No more of this," and found out who was the best doctor in the country to help his son. Now, I don't know if I am or not, but he came to see me. When we scanned his son, he had a pattern in the brain that is awful for Ritalin. Just awful! Ritalin will make this worse 8 times out of 10. I put him on a handful of supplements, got him to exercise and take fish oil. It was like a miracle! Now I've seen the son, the dad and the grandfather because these things run in families and when one person gets better you usually end up seeing the whole family.

DS- If ADD is in the family, a parent is probably going to have it and maybe 50% of the children will have it. Do you need to treat the whole family?

DA- If one parent has it, 60% of their kids will have it. If two parents have it, 90% of their kids will have it. I always tell my colleagues that the best way to build an adult psychiatric practice is to see children. Because then you'll see their parents. If you bring your child to our clinic we'll automatically screen the mom and dad. Why? Because it's not helpful to send an ADD child home with a mother who can't concentrate. Or a dad who's so impulsive that he beats the children instead of correctly disciplining them. So, yes, I think you should treat the whole family when dealing with ADD, anxiety, and depression.

DS- So if a person is looking at their own life and trying to better their life, is it wise for them to try to see the patterns in their mom, dad, uncles or aunts, grandfathers or grandmothers?

DA- Family history is a huge part. When I do an evaluation on someone, I don't just go and take a look at their brain and then give them treatment. We take the pictures but we also understand the person. So, I want to understand your grandparents, your parents, your aunts and uncles, because it will give me some clues. If you come into my office and look very ADD but you have four manic-depressive aunts and uncles, before I give you a stimulant, I want to make sure you don't have bipolar disorder because that stimulant might trigger you into a bad place.

CHAPTER ELEVEN

How To Convince Your Family To Get Help

Interview Between Rev. Don Stewart (DS)
& Dr. Daniel Amen (DA)

DS- Dr. Amen, sometimes a person needs help or may have come to realize they need help but maybe their family is not going to understand them. Perhaps family members will tell them, "You don't need help. You just need to get a hold of yourself and snap out of that mood." What does a person do when they're in a situation like that?

DA- It's very common. Most of our society still doesn't understand that depression is a brain problem, or that ADD is a brain problem. The first thing is that if you can know it yourself, that's important. And I encourage people to pop onto my link on your website – www.donstewarttv.com and they can take a free test on how their brain works to see if they're more likely to have ADD, anxiety, or depression. Give your parents, spouse, children and other family members, short books to show them that the latest medical opinions are classifying depression as a medical illness, almost like heart disease.

DS- When people understand that depression is like heart disease won't that help take away the stigma?

DA- Yes. This will help decrease the stigma that has long been associated with these illnesses. But you know, most often the stigma is within ourselves. Once a person realizes they need help, there are a lot of ways to get it. If they can't afford it, the local community health center often will provide free mental health evaluations if they need it. There is an abundance of good information that they can read in books or get off our website to get help. It's available and there's much less stigma in the US than in other places in the world.

DS- Is it harder to help some people in other cultures?

DA- Cultural issues are very important.

DR. AMEN AND CHILD PSYCHOLOGY:

DA- I'm a child psychiatrist as well, and I did my psychology training in Hawaii. Hawaii has a huge Oriental population. Those families are often very closed and private. Someone needs to be hearing voices or believing very crazy delusional things before a family realizes they need to get help. You don't want to get to that point of struggling before you take the time to get help for them.

ADD AND DEPRESSION:

DS- Now back to this single mother. She lives in the inner city, having a tough time paying her bills, her husband left her with the kids, they're with the wrong crowd, and she's depressed. What does she do? I mean, she calls my television program, and I pray for her. I get all kinds of reports from people that I pray for and it helps them. I love reading letters from them because I correspond with them. Listen to this one:

> ***"Right now, the last letter I received from you I was so depressed, but your letter brought me HOPE!"***

I wonder what happens to a brain when all of a sudden that person gets HOPE? Do you think there's some brain change going on?

THE BRAIN AND HOPE:

DA- Absolutely! Hope can activate some of the mood centers in the brain. When I believe that I am going to get better, I'm more likely to get better!

DS- And then, of course, I pray for all these people and I get prayer requests from different people. It's amazing to me the number of people that are on the verge of suicide. They write to me and ask, "What do I do?" I believe all healing comes from God; and I have no doubt as to the gift that God has given you. I have to give credit to Oral Roberts who many years ago brought medical science and prayer together.

Believe me, at that time when people were praying for the sick, that idea was way out there as far as many who believed in healing were concerned. Oral Roberts was taking a very bold step by doing that. I believe prayer and HOPE and using a Biblical Touch Point to help people develop their faith can bring healing to people. We know that medicine and doctors can help people; sometimes vitamins and other supplements can help. Are there other practical things that can help?

THE BRAIN AND ALCOHOL:

DA- Well, if I'm that single mother in the inner city, and I'm feeling depressed, and I'm reaching out to you, reaching out to her friends, reaching out to her family, there's a treatment called **"Interpersonal Therapy."** It's where we teach people to get along better with other people in their lives. That's why forgiveness works in their lives, when they don't hold on to the hurts anymore. Interpersonal Therapy has been found to be as effective as anti-depressant medication. What I would say to that woman is:

1. **Reach out to the people that you know.**
2. **Take good care of your brain!**
3. **Stop poisoning your brain.**

So, if you're drinking, you need to stop because you're only going to get worse. Half the people, who kill themselves, do it when they're drunk. So if you're depressed, the last thing you want to do is drink alcohol. Take good care of your brain because it ultimately takes care of your mood! Exercise, and learn new things. If you can afford it, you should take a multi-vitamin and fish oil every day.

AUTOMATIC NEGATIVE THOUGHTS:

DS- What part does negative thinking play in depression? Are there some methods or therapies that someone can use to help overcome depressing thoughts?

DA- I always say, "Never believe all the thoughts your brain throws at you." When people get depressed they get infested with **"Automatic Negative Thoughts."** Automatic Negative Thoughts are thoughts that just come into your mind automatically and they ruin your day. What they don't teach you in school that they should teach is that your thoughts can lie! You don't have to believe every thought that goes through your head. When you feel sad, when you feel mad, when you're feeling nervous, write out the thoughts that you're thinking. **Journaling is so helpful!** Write it out and then ask yourself, "Is this true?" And often what you'll find is that it's not true, and you're lying to yourself. We teach kids Geometry. How much Geometry have you used since the tenth grade? But we never teach them how to question their own thoughts in a systematic way.

DEVELOP AN "ANT EATER":

DA- I tell people they have to build an internal **"Ant Eater"** so whenever they're sad, mad, or nervous they need to take care of those negative thoughts. Later in the book, we have a chapter in the book specifically dealing with **"ANTS."**

DS- I think that will help a lot of people. That may be one of the reasons why we teach people to stand on the Word of God, stand on the Bible and to quote Scripture when they're going through things. In a sense, they're talking back to those negative thoughts.

DA- Yes, you're right!

DS- In a sense, they're saying, "God, I can be this person, I can do this, I can do ALL things through Christ that strengthens me!" And you're facing all this trouble and all this worry and you just hold on to this Scripture, "I can do ALL things through Christ!" You're talking back to that obstacle with God's promise and God's Word. Right?

DA- Yes. Philippians 4:8 states; *"Think on whatsoever things are true, lovely, just, pure, of good report and worthy of praise...."*

THE BRAIN AND THE SOUL:

DS- You come from a good solid Catholic background. Let's talk about the First Pope. Do you think maybe he had ADD?

DA- Peter? Peter seemed to say things impulsively. . .

DS- And do things impulsively!

DA- And do things impulsively. He cut off a soldier's ear impulsively.

DS- So, it's a possibility.

DA- Yes. "Do you know this guy? No I don't know him." This was sort of an impulsive denial that I think he regretted.

DS- I wonder what the Scripture means when it says, "*Let this mind be in you, which was also in Christ Jesus.*" Could that be interpreted, let this "brain" be in you?

DA- The mind and the brain go hand in hand.

DS- Could this mean to give yourself a "healthy brain" in a sense?

DA- Yes, one of the most interesting things that I found when I started doing the imaging work, is that when I would balance someone's brain, they became more loving; they became more easy to connect with, more thoughtful, more effective, and more hopeful. It began to really bother me in a sense because I started wondering, "What's the soul of this person really like? Are they really this person?" When I first meet them, they're this dark, evil, terrible person. Or, are they really who they are when their brain works right? What I've come to believe is that our brains are made for us to be happy, for us to be effective, to be social and connected. But when they're diseased or damaged, that's when we have problems with spousal abuse; we have problems with substance abuse. I hear people say, "Oh that's just a high tech excuse for bad behavior." My response is, "Get out of the 17th Century!" It was René Descartes who separated the mind from the brain and he was wrong! When your brain works right, you work right; when your brain has trouble, you have trouble in your life!

Chapter Twelve

Healing The Hardware Of The Soul

Interview Between Rev. Don Stewart (DS)
& Dr. Daniel Amen (DA)

DS- I love the book that you wrote, "*Healing The Hardware Of The Soul.*" I believe everyone dealing with this now needs to get this book! I love that term. I think it helps people who are going through depression to realize that they have a brain that's sick, just like a gallbladder gets sick, or eyes that need glasses, or ears that need a hearing aid. If the brain is not functioning right, then your soul is not functioning right.

BRAIN FACTS:

DA- Let's just talk about that.

Your brain is about 3 pounds.

It's 2% of your body's weight.

Your brain uses 20 – 30% of the calories that you consume, and of the blood flow of the body.

It's estimated that we have a 100 billion nerve cells connected. There are more connections in our brain than the stars in the universe.

Your brain is stunning in its complexity! It's true that your brain is involved in everything you do and when it works right, you work right, and when your brain is in trouble, you're in trouble.

DS- Describe the brain for us.

DA- It's the most complex, special, and complicated organ in the universe. It is also very soft. Did you know that your brain has the consistency of soft butter? Tofu, custard, and somewhere between there, egg whites and Jell-O. But you don't feel that because it's in a hard skull. Most people think of the brain as fixed, firm, and rubbery. That's not how it is in real life. That's how it is once it's been fixed in formaldehyde. But your brain is the consistency of custard. It is housed in a very hard skull and the skull has ridges.

THE BRAIN AND SPORTS:

DA- Knowing that, why would we ever let a child hit a soccer ball with their head? How stupid is that? We don't in any way honor the brain in our society. I live in Newport Beach, California and it's often called the "OC," or the "Plastic Society," because we have more plastic walking around in Orange County than anywhere in the world. I always say, "We care more about our faces, our boobs, our bellies and our butts, than we do about our brain!" How crazy is that? You can change the outside but things really won't change until you change the inside.

ADD AND ANXIETY:

DS- Let's talk about anxiety a little bit. What is anxiety? How would you describe it?

DA- There's healthy anxiety and then there's unhealthy anxiety. Anxiety is that part of the body, it's natural and wired in, we call it "Fight or Flight Response." It was part of our ancestors. When a caveman saw a saber-toothed tiger, immediately his brain said, "This could be trouble." Immediately, our hearts beat faster; our hands start to sweat; we get cold; we start to breathe in a different way; we get ready to fight the tiger or run! So it's normal and you need to have some anxiety. That's why you don't drive 125 miles an hour down the freeway in the rain because your brain will tell you it's not going be a good thing that happens to you. I don't need to do that. When anxiety becomes abnormal it's like you get that "fight or flight" feeling in situations that are not dangerous for you. I've read that one of the worst fears people have is speaking in front of a large group. Your heart starts to race, your hands start to sweat and get cold. I used to have terrible anxiety over public speaking. In fact, when I would get up I would never hold anything in my hands because if I did, they would just shake so bad. Thank God, that's gone away from me but it really torments some people.

THE DIFFERENCE BETWEEN ANXIETY AND FEAR:

DS- What's the difference between anxiety and fear?

DA- Fear can just be a normal thing. Pathological anxiety is when it gets over the top. It can prevent you from sleeping; it can prevent you from going out of your house. There's something called "Agoraphobia." People are so afraid of experiencing an embarrassing panic attack in public that they don't leave their house. I treated one woman who hadn't left her house in 40 years! She heard about the imaging that we did and it took all of her strength for her to get out of her house and come to our clinic to get a scan. You could see evidence of it on her scan, and with treatment, she got better. It was so exciting!

Chapter Thirteen

Obsessive Compulsive Disorder

Interview Between Rev. Don Stewart (DS) & Dr. Daniel Amen (DA)

DS- Is there any connection to anxiety and obsessive compulsive disorder?

DA- Anxiety can take the form of "Obsessive Compulsive Disorder." You get the same thought in your head over and over again. You have to wash your hands or take showers repeatedly. If you don't, you're just so worried that something bad will happen to you. It affects people physically. They have tummy aches, headaches. They can't get their breath. There are many different forms and symptoms of Obsessive Compulsive Disorder.

DS- Where does anxiety show up when you do a brain scan? Does it show up in one place or in several places?

DA- It can show up in the "Basil Ganglia." When they work too hard, people tend to be anxious, tense and nervous. On my personal brain scan it shows up as too anxious. Before I really got control of this thing, I was the kind of person that if something bad almost happened, I would play it out. So, I ended up with a lot of tummy aches, neck aches and headaches. If I was almost in a car accident I wouldn't say, "Oh thank God I wasn't in that accident." My brain would actually see the car hit me, see the windshield being broken, and see the car catch on fire. I mean my brain would actually play out all this craziness. No wonder I would feel anxious or feel in fear. Now when I see that happening and I can just stop it, by telling myself, "That's not helpful, don't go there." I now have better control over my thoughts. I don't allow them to take over. We talked about ANTS earlier – "Automatic Negative Thoughts." People with anxiety disorders are masterful at fortune telling…predicting the worst possible thing and then making it worse.

GUILT BEATING ANTS:

DS- I always thought of myself as being a very positive person. After I went to your clinic, I realized that some of the things that would come out of me concerning myself made a lot of people think, "He's humble and he's nice." But sometimes it was pretty negative stuff. I was down on myself a little bit. A little of that is good because, you don't come across as a total egomaniac. But I found myself putting myself down a little bit without realizing it. That was really brought to light when I started noticing my thought patterns. For instance, I got rid of one word that isn't even in my vocabulary anymore. Instead of saying, "I *should* have done this or I *should* have done that," I have replaced it with "I *could* have done this." Just a little change like that makes a significant difference in how you feel afterwards.

DA- Yes. They're one kind of ANT and we call them, **"Guilt Beating Ants."** We have a whole chapter in this book dedicated to the topic of **"ANTS."**

DS- So, I believe God uses prayer and faith. He uses the Anointing and the Holy Spirit to help heal people. We can stand on God's Word for answers. We know there are certain medications that help people. What are some other ways or tools that people can use to help them?

A "BRAIN HEALTHY LIFE":

DA- We should talk about a "Brain Healthy Life." We have a chapter late in the book telling you about the **"Nine Principles To A Healthy Brain."** The first thing in a "Brain Healthy Life" is you want to protect your brain. Head injuries do matter. The brain is soft, the skull is hard. Stop hitting soccer balls with your head or letting your kids do that. Stop playing tackle football or riding motorcycles or not wearing seat belts. Stop getting drunk because you're more likely to get a head injury when you're drunk either from a car accident or a fight or falling down or whatever.

Protect your brain. Stop poisoning it. Drugs, alcohol, some medications like pain or anti-anxiety medications, are not very good for the brain. Smoking is terrible for the brain because it constricts blood flow. We can tell which are smokers because we can actually see their skin. It's prematurely aged. So the same thing is going on in the brain.

DS- What about coffee?

DA- Limit your caffeine usage. Caffeine prematurely ages you as it constricts blood flow to the brain and certain organs as well. Get enough sleep. People who get less than seven hours of sleep at night have lower overall blood flow to their brain. As a society, in 1900 we got, on an average, about nine hours of sleep at night. In 2007, we get an average of six hours of sleep at night. No wonder the incidents of ADD and depression have gone up so much. We're not allowing our brains enough time to recharge so we have to have that cup of coffee in the morning. Why? Because we're sleep deprived. We need a little alcohol at night. Why? To settle us down because we had too much coffee during the day. So we're using uppers and downers – not great for our brain.

DS- So we need to protect our brain.

DIET AND EXERCISE:

DA- Yes, we need to protect our brain. We need to have a healthy brain so the first thing is, don't hurt it. The second thing is you have to eat healthy. We have such terrible nutrition in this country. We are the wealthiest country on the planet and it's a shame to have such awful nutrition. We have "fast food diet," because we're running way too fast. Good diet is lean protein. You need protein. Low protein diets are a disaster for brain function. All the hundred billions of nerve cells you have are made up of protein. Complex carbohydrates – get rid of all the simple sugars. I was just in New York and I love the M&M's store. Not good for your brain. Complex carbohydrates! I tell people to eat from the rainbow, which means foods with many different colors because they have lots of antioxidants and that does not mean Skittles. I do not mean Skittles candy! Decrease bad fat.

DS- What about Omega 3 fatty acids?

DA- We need Omega 3 fatty acids for our brains to work right. In fact, it's found in fish and in fish oil. Omega 3 fatty acids are found to be low in depression, low in ADD, low in dementia, and low in people who try to kill themselves. Taking fish oil on a regular basis has been found to be good for the heart, good for your skin, eyes, joints, hair, and good for your brain. I think, every day, we should take a 100% multi-vitamin because we don't have balanced diets, and we should be taking grey fish oil. Work to eat from the rainbow with good protein and good fats. Good fats come from fish, avocados, walnuts, canola oil, and olive oil – and get rid of trans fats because they are poison to the brain.

So protect your brain, eat right, and exercise. Why? Because it keeps you young. I'm interested in living to one hundred. I like my life. I really want the "Fountain of Youth." Research says it can be found in physical exercise. In fact, there's a head-to-head study with exercise and Zoloft. Zoloft is one of our very good anti-depressants like Prozac. Head to head after twelve weeks: equally effective. After twelve weeks of Zoloft, what you have is your insurability is not as good because you've been taking an anti-depressant. There are sexual side effects from the anti-depressant, also. After twelve weeks of exercise, you have a better body, it doesn't affect your insurability, and you're more likely to have a better brain because you have better blood flow. At ten months, after taking Zoloft, exercise beat the socks off of Zoloft. Exercise improves blood flow to the brain. Why is blood flow so important? Because it brings oxygen, sugar, nutrients, and it takes away the toxic things that happen in your brain. It's incredible. Blood flow is critical. Whatever is good for the heart is good for the brain. Whatever is bad for the heart is bad for the brain.

DS- I saw you have a new book, "*Sex On The Brain.*" What's that all about?

DA- I have a new book in the bookstores, it's called ***"Sex On The Brain."*** In it, I explain that whatever is good for the heart is good for the brain. Also, whatever is good for the genitals from a blood-flow standpoint, is good for your heart, and is good for the brain. Most people don't know that 40% of 40 year olds, have erectile dysfunction. My goodness, that should worry people!

DS- That's why you see all that stuff advertised on TV?

THE KEY TO THE FOUNTAIN OF YOUTH:

DA- Yes. It's everywhere. About 70% of 70 year olds have erectile dysfunction. If you want the "Fountain of Youth," then keep up your daily exercising to keep the blood flow maximized. It's good for your sexual function, which is very important to your health.

DS- It's all a matter of blood flow? The Bible says ". . . *the life of a creature is in the blood* . . ." Leviticus 17:11 (New International Version)

DA- Yes. It's all a matter of blood flow. Anything that hurts blood flow – diabetes, caffeine, nicotine, heart disease, hypertension, terrible diet – are more likely to make you depressed. You are more likely to have heart problems and sexual-function problems. Exercise is clearly the fountain of youth. The best exercise is coordination exercises, like dancing or tennis. Table tennis is my favorite. Along with exercise comes mental exercise – new learning. Whenever you learn something new, your brain makes a new connection. When you stop learning, the brain actually starts unraveling itself. So we should exercise 15-20 minutes every day. We should also be learning something new for 15-20 minutes a day, whether it's a new language or studying your Bible. But, it has to be new to you. If you're doing the same thing like studying the Book of John for the eighteenth time, it's probably not the greatest thing for your brain because your brain's not being challenged. It's something that has to be a new skill for you!

DS- You know I remember the times that I have really been into exercise in a consistent way, I get my heart rate up and it helps my ADD. I can concentrate and function a lot better.

DA- A lot of people say, "I can't take medicine" or "I don't want to take medicine." "Are there natural treatments for ADD, anxiety, and depression?" You bet there are, and it starts with exercise. Exercise boosts blood flow to the brain. Exercise boosts certain neuro-transmitters to the brain, and if you want the other natural treatments for ADD, it's intense exercise and fish oil. Fish oil is a key in helping the brain work better. A higher protein, lower carbohydrate diet is key. Get rid of the simple sugars in the diet and you'll be able to concentrate so much better! I treat pilots – and you know that if pilots take medicine, then they can't fly. They always need the "natural" treatment. There are certain supplements that I talk about on my website and in my books that can be a useful resource.

Chapter Fourteen

Physical Healing For ADD

Interview Between Rev. Don Stewart (DS) & Dr. Daniel Amen (DA)

DS- I really believe that all healing comes from God. He uses all kinds of methods to heal people. He uses the medical profession. He uses vitamins and herbs. He uses health remedies. He uses prayer and faith, and He can use a combination of all these things. I think that's what Jesus meant when He came to the paralyzed man at the pool of Bethesda and said, "*Will you be made whole?*" I think what God is wanting us to come into is wholeness. He wants us to be made complete individuals. And I don't think we can be that way if we don't have healthy brains, can we?

DA- Absolutely not.

ANT EATERS FOR ANTS:

DS- Lets talk about the ANTS or Automatic Negative Thoughts that come into our minds. I have a little stuffed animal of an anteater here and you teach that you need to talk back to these negative thoughts. This anteater reminds me to eat up those negative thoughts when they come into my head.

CHEMICALS RELEASED FROM THOUGHTS:

DA- You need to have an internal anteater. Every time you have a thought, your brain releases chemicals. Every single time. Whenever you have bad thoughts, hopeless thoughts – any negative thought that you have – your body produces a set of chemicals that make you feel awful. And, the opposite is true. Whenever you have a happy thought, a hopeful thought, or a loving thought your brain releases a completely different set of chemicals that make you feel good. In fact, I have an exercise I teach my patients about gratitude. I have them focus on five things a day that you are grateful for. We actually found that it has antidepressant qualities when you focus on what you love about life instead of what you hate about life.

HAVING CONTROL OF YOUR THOUGHTS:

DS- What do we do about the negative thoughts that come to us?

DA- Thoughts are automatic. We don't have control over all the thoughts that come into our mind. They're based on memories and complex chemical reactions. But what most people don't know is that THOUGHTS LIE! THEY LIE A LOT! You don't have to believe every thought that you have just because you have a thought. That has nothing to do with whether or not it's true. If you really want to gain control over your moods in order to be happy and be better, then you have to correct the negative thoughts that come into your mind.

One day I was working with a patient and he was depressed and had all these negative thoughts and I was just thinking, "this guy is just infested with ANTS!" That night when I came home, we had an infestation in the kitchen with ants; they were everywhere! They were climbing on the walls, crawling out of the light sockets, climbing all over the pantry, and as I was cleaning up thousands of ants I realized that the ANTS, or Automatic Negative Thoughts, were like my patient at work today. He was infested. I said, "he needs RAID". Then I thought, that's not a good analogy since I work with children. Then I thought anteater! So I got an ant puppet and an anteater puppet and started working with 8 year olds and 12 year olds and they loved it! They loved the analogy that you don't have to believe every thought that you have. You can take the anteater and eat the bad thoughts and get rid of these negative things. So whenever you feel sad, mad, or nervous, write out what's going on in your head and talk back to it! I don't know if when you were a teenager you ever talked back but I was an expert! My dad will tell you today that, "Daniel can talk back!" But we never talk back to ourselves.

DS- Now when we talk back to these ANTS, does something happen in our brain? Has that ever been measured? Do you take a scan and see the results?

DA- Absolutely. We kick in the best part of our brain, which is the front part of our brain, and it starts taking over positive control for us. For instance, the negative part of my brain is telling me: *"This program that we're doing together isn't going to work."* My supervising side of the brain is telling me: *"What? Are you kidding me? This is going to be great fun! We're going to work on this together. We have two bright, smart, fun, caring people who are going to make this work."* But if I listen to the part of my brain telling me, *"This isn't going to work,"* then I might not even do it. Those negative thoughts control people's lives.

DS- That would be like having the negative thoughts of, *"You know, here you are Don; you minister to people, you pray for*

people, you operate in the Gifts of the Spirit, and they're not going to listen to a shrink; they're not going to listen to a psychiatrist." This is a thought that might come into my brain. I had to tell myself, ***"NO! These people are just like me. This is going to make sense to them, because it made sense to me. I've gone through these same things that they have to deal with."***

REV. STEWART'S BATTLES OF DEPRESSION:

DS- I have had two depressions in my life that I'm aware of. One was probably a delayed grief, where I lost my mentor and my father within a couple of months of each other. But I was so busy that I had to drown those feelings and keep everything going. It didn't hit me until two or three years later when I went through this grieving, depressed time. I'm sure it was some kind of delayed grief.

There was another time, and I don't even know what triggered it. I started worrying, feeling guilt, anxiety, having crazy thoughts like, ***"You're not gonna make it."*** Stuff that was unlike how I normally feel. I thought, ***"You know, the people that I minister to are going through these same things, and I need to bring knowledge and understanding to them along with the Gift that God has given to me."***

You know, Dr. Amen, we're both really in the business of giving hope to people. That's what you do and that's what I do – but nobody does it better than I do – but you're good at it, too.

DA- That's right! Positive Automatic Thoughts!

DS- It makes a lot of sense to me if we can bring hope to people and give them some practical things to use.

DA- But if you would have stayed with the negative thoughts, and if you would have believed it, then you wouldn't be able to share powerful ways to help people.

DS- Well, you've probably had some thoughts about not getting associated with some wild, TV evangelist.

DA- Actually, I didn't think that. The thought I had was, "Why do I have to get up at 4:30 this morning to come to Phoenix, and do this interview?"

DS- I have ADD – I don't call it Attention Deficit Disorder. I call it "Always Developing Destinies through God's grace." The other name that is used is ADHD – Attention Deficit Hyperactive Disorder. I call it "Always Developing HOPEFUL Destinies." I've had an effective ministry for over 48 years. God took a weakness and made it strong. "Let the weak say, I am strong." Joel 3:10 (New International Version)

CHAPTER FIFTEEN

ANT Eaters: Talk To Your Thoughts And Change Them!

Rev. Don Stewart & Dr. Amen

Rev. Don Stewart

A verse in the Bible that has given me understanding is found in **Ephesians 4:23, *"Be renewed in the spirit of your mind."***

The word ***renewed*** comes from the Greek word ***ananeoo*** which means "to renovate or reform; renew." The word ***spirit*** here comes from the Greek word ***pneuma*** which means "mental disposition, attitude, the rational soul."

Renovate or restore your soul. Rebuild or remodel your soul. David said in Psalm 23:3, "He restoreth my soul." In other words, I have my thoughts straightened out. Here is the exciting thing to me – we can change our brain, which is the hardware of our souls. Through Dr. Amen's brain imaging you can actually see the changes that can be made by changing our thoughts and our words.

***"As a man thinks in his heart, so is he..."* Proverbs 23:7**

The Bible is very clear about the power of our thoughts and words. You become what you think. Look at the power of your words. ***"Death and life are in the power of the tongue..."* Proverbs 18:21**

Jesus said ***"If you have faith as a grain of mustard seed, you will say to this mountain, 'Move from here to there,' and it will move; and nothing will be impossible for you."* Matthew 17:20**

"...let the weak say, I am strong." **Joel 3:10**

You are strong because, ***"You can do all things through Christ who strengthens you."*** **Philippians 4:13**

We must learn to, ***"Resist the devil and he will flee from us."*** **James 4:7** Our biggest battle is in the battleground of our mind.

In Matthew 4, just before Jesus started His public ministry, He went into the wilderness and fasted for 40 days. After which He was tempted of the devil in three ways. The tempter came to Him and said:

1) "If you are the Son of God, command these stones be made bread."

Jesus talked back and said ***"<u>It is written</u>, 'Man shall not live by bread alone, but by every word that proceeds from the mouth of God.'"*** **Matthew 4:4**

2) The devil took Him up on a pinnacle of the Temple and said "If You are the Son of God, throw Yourself down. For <u>it is written:</u> ***'He shall give His angels charge over you,'"*** Matthew 4:6

Jesus answered. He talked to him (**His thoughts**). He said **"<u>It is written</u> again, *'You shall not tempt the LORD your God.'"*** **Matthew 4:7**

3) The devil took Him to a high mountain and said to Him ***"All these things I will give You if You will fall down and worship me."*** **Matthew 4:8,9**

Jesus talked back again and said ***"'You shall worship the LORD your God and Him only you shall serve.'"*** **Matthew 4:10**

Then the Bible says in Matthew 4:11 ***"The devil left Him, and, behold, angels came and ministered to Him."***

This may be the most important thing to understand when you are dealing with ADD, anxiety, or depression. **Your biggest battle is going to take place in your thought life.** Learn from what Jesus did.

First, talk back using the principles in the Word of God. Jesus said "It is written." There is power in using the Word of God to talk back. It doesn't make any difference if you use a Bible verse verbatim or use the principle that is taught in the Bible.

The second thing is that in all three temptations the little two letter word *IF* is used. You can see the biggest temptation that Christ had was His self-doubt. ***"If you are the Son of God...."*** It was not being hungry. It was an attack on His identity. This is what happens in anxiety, depression, and ADD. Think of it like this: if Jesus, the Son of God, had to deal with thoughts of *IF*, thoughts of doubt, then you as a Christian are not above dealing with thoughts of doubt or identity temptations. That's why it's so important to know who you are in Christ.

You and I have to deal with the same type of temptations every day. IF. Things like "IF you're so smart, why are you so stupid?" "IF you are so gifted and have all that talent, why can't you ever finish anything?" "IF you are really a Christian why are you even having these kind of thoughts?" Dr. Amen, as a neuroscientist as well as a child psychiatrist, developed an analogy to help children as well as adults called ANTS or Automatic Negative Thoughts. We all have Automatic Negative Thoughts, but what is most important is how we deal with them. I have in my office as well as my home a little stuffed anteater – to remind me to destroy all the ants that come into my mind.

Dr. Amen is going to give you an overview of what he calls ANTS. Although he does not necessarily use Bible terminology, they are all Bible-based principles that work. At the end of each ANT, I will give you my perception from the Bible, if you would like to use Bible terminology.

Dr. Amen

People who have anxiety or depression often develop erroneous thought patterns, based on the failures they have experienced in their lives. It often helps to investigate the way this person thinks and then teach him or her to correct any erroneous thought patterns.

Here are some examples of common negative thoughts:

"I'm a terrible student."

"I'm always messing things up."

"No one ever wants to be with me."

"Anybody could have done that. I'm not so special."

"The boss (or teacher) doesn't like me."

"I will fail at this."

"I feel you don't love me."

"I should do better."

"I'm so stupid."

These thoughts severely limit a person's ability to enjoy his or her life. How people think "moment by moment" has a huge impact on how they feel and how they behave. Negative thoughts often drive difficult behaviors and cause people to have problems with their self-esteem. Hopeful thoughts, on the other hand, influence positive behaviors and lead people to feel good about themselves and be more effective in their day-to-day lives.

In many ways our brain works like a computer. When a person receives negative input about themselves, they store it in their subconscious mind, and the input becomes expressed as negative thoughts, feelings, or behaviors. Unless people are taught how to talk back to these harmful thoughts and messages, they believe them unconditionally. This is a critical point. Most people never challenge the thoughts that go through their heads. They never even think about their own thoughts. They just believe what they think, even though the thoughts may be very irrational. Their behavior is therefore based on false assumptions or false ideas.

Why do we spend so much time teaching kids about diagramming sentences and geometry and so little time teaching them how to think clearly? Most people do not understand how important thoughts are and leave the development of thought patterns to random chance. Did you know that thoughts have actual weight and mass? They are real! They have significant influence on every cell in your body. When a person's mind is burdened with many negative thoughts, it affects that person's ability to learn, his or her ability to relate to other people, and his or her physical health. Teaching people with anxiety and depression how to control and direct their thoughts in a positive way can be helpful in all areas of their lives.

Here are step-by-step "positive thinking" principles that I use in my psychotherapy practice with children, teens, and adults. When people truly learn these principles, they gain more control over their feelings and their behavior.

This is what happens every time you have a thought.

Step #1: Every time you have a thought, your brain releases chemicals.

That's how our brain works:

- You have a thought
- Your brain releases chemicals
- An electrical transmission goes across your brain, and...
- You become aware of what you're thinking.

Thoughts are real and they have a real impact on how you feel and how you behave.

Step #2: Every time you have a mad thought, an unkind thought, a sad thought, or a cranky thought,

your brain releases negative chemicals that make your body feel bad.

Think about the last time you were mad. What did you feel inside your body? When most people are mad, their muscles get tense, their hearts beat faster, their hands start to sweat, and they may even begin to feel a little dizzy. Your body reacts to every negative thought you have.

Step #3: Every time you have a good thought, a happy thought, a hopeful thought, or a kind thought, your brain releases chemicals that make your body feel good.

Think about the last time you had a really happy thought (such as when you got a good grade on a test or cuddled a child). What did you feel inside your body? When most people are happy their muscles relax, their hearts beat slower, their hands become dry, and they breathe slower. Your body also reacts to your good thoughts.

Step #4: Your body reacts to every thought you have! We know this from polygraphs, or lie detector tests. During a lie detector test, you are hooked up to equipment that measures:

- Hand Temperature
- Heart Rate
- Blood Pressure
- Breathing Rate
- Muscle Tension
- How Much The Hands Sweat

The tester then asks questions, such as, "Did you do that thing?" If you did the bad thing, your body is likely to have a "Stress" response and it is likely to react. Now the opposite is also true. If you did not do what they are asking you about, it is likely that your body will experience a "relaxation" response and will react.

Again, almost immediately your body reacts to what you think. This not only happens when you're asked about telling the truth, your body reacts to every thought you have, whether it is about school, work, friends, family, or anything else. Now let's look at the nine Automatic Negative Thoughts (ANTS).

ANT #1: "ALWAYS" THINKING

These ANTS occur when you over generalize a situation and think something that happened once will "always" repeat itself. For example, if your wife snaps at you, you may think, "She's always irritable," even though she may only have snapped once. The thought, "She's always irritable" is so negative that it makes you feel sad and upset. It activates your limbic system, which is a part of your brain. Whenever you think in absolutes such as "always," "never," "no one," "everyone," "every time," or "everything," you are engaging in negative thinking that seems to make a temporary situation a permanent reality. Here are some examples of "always" thinking:

"He's *always* angry."
"*No one* is concerned about my ideas."
"He *never* listens to me."
"*Everyone* takes advantage of me."
"You turn away *every time* I touch you."
"My kids *always* disrespect me."

"Always thinking" ANTS are very common. Beware when they creep into your thinking (and conversations) as they can have a very negative effect on your mood, attitude, and relationships.

Rev. Don Stewart

During the times in my life when it seemed that my whole world was caving in I told myself that things are never as bad as it seemed at the time. The Word of God says:

> ***"For our light affliction, which is but for a moment...For the things which are seen are temporary..."* 2 Corinthians 4:17-18**

It is so easy to fall in the trap of thinking "I'll never get out of this situation." This is the time for you to hope. Some time ago one of my friends from Canada, Ruby, said to me, "Don, God is never going to forgive me for all I've done." She began to tell me about all the things she did when she was healthy and now she was sick. I said to her, "the first thing we have to do is get rid of the word *never*." I told her about God's grace and how we can't make God love us. He just loves us. I could see hope rise in her. I gave her the Scripture:

> ***"Now may the God of hope fill you with all joy and peace in believing, that you may abound in hope, by the power of the Holy Spirit."* Romans 15:13**

She said it out loud several times and her whole countenance lit up. Hope is your medicine – your joy and peace.

Dr. Amen

ANT #2: "FOCUSING ON THE NEGATIVE"

These ANTS occur when you focus only on what's going wrong in a situation and ignore everything that could be construed as positive. This ANT can take a positive experience, relationship, or work interaction and taint it with negativity. For example, you feel a deep desire to help a neighbor in need and you have the means and knowledge to help, but as you prepare to step in, you remember a time when the neighbor disappointed you. Even though you have had many positive encounters with your neighbor, you become focused on the negative event. The negativity causes you to pause in your effort to help, and then you get distracted by other things and forget to help.

Your deep limbic system can learn a powerful lesson from the Disney movie *Pollyanna*. In the movie, Pollyanna goes to live with her aunt after the death of her missionary parents. Although an orphan, Pollyanna is able to help many "negative people" with her positive attitude when she introduces them to the "glad game" her father taught her. Pollyanna first played the glad game when her parents requested a doll for her from their missionary sponsors and mistakenly received crutches instead. Rather than be upset at not having a doll, Pollyanna's father taught her she could be glad because they didn't need crutches. This very simple game changes the attitudes and lives of many people in the movie. Pollyanna has a particular effect on the unhappy "hell and damnation" minister. Pollyanna tells him that her father said there were 800 "glad" passages in the Bible and that if God mentioned being glad that many times, it must be because He wants us to think that way.

Focusing on the negative in situations will make you feel bad. Playing the glad game, or looking for the positive, will help you feel better.

Rev. Don Stewart

The Word of God gives us very clear instructions about how we should think and what we should think about. God knows that this negative type of thinking is harmful to us, so He says in His Word that:

> ***"...whatsoever things are true... honest... just... pure... lovely... are of good report; if there be any virtue, and if there be any praise, think on these things."* Philippians 4:8**

In fact, God gives us an example in the Bible to help us play our own "glad game." Not only does He want us to practice "happy thoughts" but He also gets us started by mentioning several reasons why we can have a positive outlook instead of a negative one.

> ***"Bless the Lord, O my soul, and forget not all His benefits: Who forgives all your iniquities, Who heals all your diseases, Who redeems your life from destruction, Who crowns you with loving kindness and tender mercies,"* Psalm 103:2-4**

I remember years ago in Jacksonville, Florida, in one of my tent meetings, I had people stand up and quote their favorite Scripture. Lucy who was about 80 years old at the time and one of the sweetest women I had ever met, stood up and said, "Bless the Lord, O my soul and I gets all the benefits." Well, she didn't quote the Scripture exactly right, but she didn't really change the truth of it because when you bless the Lord – or fill your soul with praise, you do get all the benefits.

Dr. Amen

ANT #3: "FORTUNE TELLING"

These ANTS occur when you predict that bad or negative things will happen. I call them Fortune-telling ANTS. They underlie most anxiety disorders, especially with people who have panic attacks. Predicting the worst in a situation causes an immediate rise in heart and breathing rates. Having these thoughts can make you feel tense. When you predict that bad things will happen, you may find yourself experiencing them. If, for example, you are driving to work and you predict that you'll have a bad day, the first bad thing that happens will reinforce your belief and the rest of the day will go downhill. While it's important to be prepared for potential negative events or outcomes, over focusing on them will damage your peace of mind and ultimately ruin your health.

I have struggled with fortune-telling ANTS throughout my life. I know how they can cause a pervasive sense of fear and anxiety. When I first started my brain imaging research, I decided to study the brain patterns of my own family, including my mother, my aunt, my wife, my three children, and myself. I wanted to see if the patterns I was seeing correlated with the people with whom I had the most intimate knowledge. I quickly learned that getting my own brain scanned was not an easy experience.

Even with all that I have intellectually accomplished in my life, I was still very anxious about the procedure. What if something was wrong with my brain? What if nothing was there at all? I never felt more naked than after my scan, when my own brain activity was projected onto a computer screen in front of my colleagues. At that moment, I would rather have been without clothes than without the covering of my skull. I was relieved to see very good activity in nearly all of my brain. I saw an area of over activity in the right side of my basal ganglia, however, that stood out like a red Christmas tree light bulb. The part of the brain that often sets off anxiety was working too hard. This discovery made sense to me.

Although I do not have a clinical disorder, such as Panic Disorder, I have struggled my whole life with minor issues of anxiety. I used to bite my nails and sometimes still do when I feel anxious. I used to find it very difficult to ask for payment from patients after therapy sessions. I also had a terrible time speaking in front of large groups (which now I love to do). My first appearance on television was terrible. My hands sweated so much that I unknowingly rubbed them on my pants throughout the interview. Right before my second television interview, I nearly had a panic attack. While I was sitting in the green room waiting to go on the air, my mind became flooded with fortune-telling ANTS, and I began to predict disaster.

I thought I would make a fool of myself, forget my own

name, say something stupid, stutter or stumble over my words, and basically make an idiot of myself in front of 2 million people. Thankfully, I recognized what was happening to me and chuckled to myself: "I treat people who have this problem. Breathe with your belly and kill the ANTS."

Rev. Don Stewart

Whenever we assume that the worst is going to happen, we become anxious about the future. But **Philippians 4:6** says that we should ***"Be anxious for nothing, but in everything by prayer and supplication, with thanksgiving, let your requests be made known to God."*** In other words, don't be worried about what is going to happen in your future. Why? Because we have this promise:

***"And we know all things work together for good to them that love God, to them who are called according to His purpose."* Romans 8:28**

Any time you face the temptation to believe that your future holds only negative things, do what Jesus would do – stand tall and say, "It is written..." because God's Word says He will lead us to success, ***"Now thanks be to God who always leads us in triumph in Christ..."* 2 Corinthians 2:14**

You can be safe and secure...***"But whoever listens to me will dwell safely, and will be secure, without fear of evil."* Proverbs 1:33**

You can accomplish everything God has for you to do. ***"I can do all things through Christ who strengthens me."* Philippians 4:13**

Nothing can keep God from loving you. ***"For I am persuaded that neither death nor life, nor angels nor principalities nor powers, nor things present nor things to come, nor height nor depth, nor any other created thing,***

shall be able to separate us from the love of God which is in Christ Jesus our Lord." **Romans 8:38-39**

Dr. Amen

ANT #4: "MIND READING"

Mind-reading ANTS occur when you think you know what others are thinking even when they haven't told you. Mind reading is a common cause of trouble between people. It frequently happens in intimate relationships because one partner assumes he can read the other's mind – but you can never know what others are thinking. You know you are mind reading when you have thoughts such as, "He doesn't like me." "They were talking about me." "They think I will never amount to much." I tell people that a negative look from someone else may be nothing more than his being constipated! You just don't know.

When there are things you don't understand, ask for clarification and stay away from mind-reading ANTS. They are very infectious and cause trouble between people.

Rev. Don Stewart

At times, when Jesus was dealing with people, the Bible says that He "knew their thoughts," and He was able to minister to them specifically. God has spiritual gifts that He gives to confirm one to minister. However, that does not mean that as humans, we can always "know" someone else's thoughts. Even we who have been gifted by God, if we are not in the spirit, can't always tell what someone else is thinking. In fact, the Book of Proverbs, which is filled with Godly wisdom, warns us about assuming we know what others are thinking. The following verses are from the Message Bible because I think it says it the best.

"Don't jump to conclusions – there may be a perfectly good explanation for what you just saw." **Proverbs 25:8**

"Don't assume that you know it all. Run to God! Run from evil!" **Proverbs 3:1**

A friend of mine, Mary, always felt she knew what I was thinking. She felt like she could read my body language and she would assume certain things that were just not true. It put a strain on our friendship. I tried to explain to her about my ADD – that there were times that I would super-focus to the point where I didn't notice if she or anyone else was around. People would think that I was mad at them, but I was just so focused on something else that I might not even hear them or see them. I would say that "I got in a zone." Sometimes I would be writing or something else. This has been a very valuable tool for me through the years.

Dr. Amen

ANT #5: "THINKING WITH YOUR FEELINGS"

These ANTS occur when you believe your negative feelings without ever questioning them. Feelings are very complex and are often based on powerful memories from the past. Feelings sometimes lie but many people believe their feelings even though they have no evidence to back them up. "Thinking with your feelings" thoughts usually start with the word "I feel." For example, "I feel like you don't love me." "I feel stupid." "I feel like a failure." "I feel nobody will ever trust me." Whenever you have a strong negative feeling, check it out. Look for evidence behind the feeling. Do you have real reasons to feel that way? Or are your feelings based on events or things from the past?

Rev. Don Stewart

When our feelings are filled with negativity, it not only hurts us emotionally, but also spiritually and physically. ***"A merry heart does good, like medicine, But a broken spirit dries the bones."*** **Proverbs 17:22**

But we can't forget the first part of the verse, because it reminds us that our health and victory are connected to our heart (our feelings and emotions). God created our emotions so we could feel His love and experience His joy. You can think of our feelings and emotions as an air duct that carries our expressions of praise and worship to His throne and carries His love and joy down to us on earth. King David knew there was a connection between how he felt and the victorious praises he gave to God. See what he had to say here: ***"Why are you cast down, O my soul? And why are you disquieted within me? Hope in God, for I shall yet praise Him."*** **Psalm 42:5**

David knew that his negative feelings were lying to him, because he said that he would praise God again, even though his feelings told him that things were bad. All he needed was to have Hope in God.

"Why does your heart carry you away?" **Job 15:12**

Ask God to help you discern your feelings, so you can know that your negative feelings are unhealthy. Then you can exchange those unhealthy feelings for the joy of your salvation.

Dr. Amen

ANT #6: "GUILT BEATINGS"

Guilt is generally not a helpful emotion, especially for your deep limbic system. In fact, guilt often causes you to do things that you don't want to do. Guilt beatings happen when you think with words like "should," "must," "ought," or "have to." Here are some examples: "I *ought* to spend more time at home." "I *must* spend more time with my kids." "I *should* have sex more often." "I *have* to organize my office." Guilt-inducing behaviors are common in many religious institutions. "Live your life this way or else bad things will happen to you" is a frequent message. Of course there are things that you should not do. Moral teaching is very important. Yet when the goal of teaching is to produce guilt, it is often counterproductive.

Unfortunately, guilt often backfires. Because of human nature, whenever we think that we "must" do something, no matter what it is, we don't want to do it. It is better to replace "guilt beatings" with phrases such as "I want to do this…" "It fits with my goals to do that…" "It would be helpful to do this…" In the examples above, it would be helpful to change those phrases to "I want to spend more time at home." "It's in our best interest for my kids and me to spend more time together." "I want to please my spouse by making wonderful love with him [or her] because he [or she] is important to me." "It's in my best interest to organize my office." Get rid of the unnecessary emotional turbulence that holds you back from achieving the goals you want.

Rev. Don Stewart

I want to give you a revelation now that I believe will set you free if you are dealing with this kind of ANT. God does not expect you to be perfect! He knows that we make mistakes and that we don't always live up to the expectations that are put on us. ***"There is therefore now no condemnation to them which are in Christ Jesus, who walk not after the flesh, but after the Spirit."* Romans 8:1**

When you have guilt in an area of your life, it can be helpful to recognize if you are trying to live up to God's standards, your own standards, or someone else's standards. If it is God's standards, remember that Jesus died to forgive you and the Holy

Spirit came to help you. So you can live the best life you can after the Spirit of God without fear of guilt or condemnation. If it is your own standards you feel guilty about, remember God created you to have choices in your life, and it is up to you to "choose" to do the important things in life. You don't have to force yourself to do it; you have the freedom to *choose* to do it.

If you are dealing with someone else's standards for you, remember that you can't make everyone happy, but you can choose what is most important for you to accomplish. Some time ago I found myself saying I should have done this or that. It dawned on me that every time I said *should* I was showering myself with guilt. We all can find reasons why maybe we should have done something differently.

Saying *should* does not help. It's like turning the shower on more, and guilt floods the soul. I replaced the word *should* with *could*. I could have done it this way. I could have made a different choice. When you say *could* instead of *should* it's like turning the shower of guilt off. If there's any change that needs to be made, saying could instead of should empowers you to make the change. ***"Guilt is banished through love and truth; Fear of God deflects evil."*** **Proverbs 16:6**

Dr. Amen

ANT #7: "LABELING"

Whenever you attach a negative label to yourself or to someone else, you prevent yourself from taking a clear look at the situation. Some examples of negative labels that people use are "jerk," "frigid," "arrogant," and "irresponsible." Negative labels are very harmful because whenever you call yourself or someone else a jerk or arrogant, you lump that person in your mind with all the "jerks" or "arrogant people" that you've ever known and you become unable to deal with them in a reasonable way. Stay away from negative labels.

Rev. Don Stewart

I think it is important to remember that whenever you speak negatively about yourself or another person, you are commenting on a human being who is infinitely precious to our Lord. The Bible says that God is love. (1 John 4:16) It also says that, ***"Love...is kind...thinks no evil:"* 1 Corinthians 13:4-5**. This means that we serve a kind God who thinks no evil toward us. So why would we want to label ourselves (or someone else) with negativity? God doesn't even do that.

The Word of God says that only looking at things from the outward appearance (or the labels we use) is not a wise thing to do. ***"Do you look at things according to the outward appearance? ...But they, measuring themselves by themselves, and comparing themselves among themselves, are not wise."* 2 Corinthians 10:7,12**

In Numbers 13, twelve men were sent to spy out the Promise Land. Ten came back with a negative report. They said, ***"There we saw the giants... and we were like grasshoppers in our own sight, and so we were in their sight."* Numbers 13:33.** They labeled themselves as weak, defeated, and like grasshoppers. Two men came back with a positive report. It was very realistic, but still positive. They said, "there are giants in the land and they are strong, but we are well able to go in and possess the land." If you label yourself as a grasshopper, people will see you the same way.

Dr. Amen

ANTS #8: "PERSONALIZATION"

Personalization occurs when innocuous events are taken personally – "My boss didn't talk to me this morning. She must be mad at me." Or, one feels he or she is the cause of all the bad things that happen – "My son got into a car accident. I should have spent more time teaching him to drive. It must be my fault." There are many other possible reasons for behavior besides the negative interpretations of a part of the brain called the limbic system. For example, your boss may not have talked to you because she was preoccupied or upset, or she was in a hurry. You never fully know why people do what they do. Try not to personalize their behavior.

Rev. Don Stewart

People with ADD, anxiety, and depression many times will take very innocent things personally. Do you know that even if it seems like everything and everybody is turning against you, you can still rejoice? You might ask "How is that possible?"

The Bible says: ***"(Love)..."rejoices in the truth."*** **1 Corinthians 13:6**

"Rejoice in the Lord always: and again I say, Rejoice." **Philippians 4:4**

Rejoicing is infectious; it will cause your heart to be merry. ***"A merry heart does good, like medicine, But a broken spirit dries the bones."*** **Proverbs 17:22**

That means you can have JOY because the TRUTH is that the things that you think are meant to hurt you are really not coming against you personally at all. God wants you to have success and be victorious, but that can be hard if you think the whole world is against you.

In **Ecclesiastes 7:21** the Bible says: ***"Also do not take to heart everything people say..."*** That's like the man who said, "I had to stop going to football games because every time the players would get in a huddle, I thought they were talking about me." Take another look at the situation and ask God to show you the truth concerning the circumstances of your life. I think you will see areas where instead of thinking that people are trying to hurt you, you will finds ways that you can reach out to those same people with God's love.

Imagine the good feelings you will have when, instead of taking something personally, you have a chance to minister God's joy and love into a hurting person's life. You will no longer have to worry about being ashamed, because you will be able to walk in perpetual deliverance. ***"For I know that this will turn out for my deliverance...according to my earnest expectation and hope that in nothing I shall be ashamed..."*** **Philippians 1:19-20**

Dr. Amen

ANT #9 BLAME (THE MOST POISONOUS ANT):

Blame is very harmful. When you blame something or someone else for the problems in your life, you become a victim of circumstances and you cannot do anything to change your situation. Many relationships are ruined by people who blame their partners when things go wrong. They take little responsibility for or won't admit to their problems. When something goes wrong at home or at work, they try to find someone to blame. Typically, you'll hear statements from them such as:

"It wasn't my fault that..."
"That wouldn't have happened if you had..."
"How was I supposed to know...?"
"It's your fault that..."

The bottom line statement goes something like this: "If only you had done something differently, I wouldn't be in the predicament I'm in. It's your fault, and I'm not responsible."

Whenever you blame someone else for the problems in your life, you become powerless to change anything. The "blame game" hurts your personal sense of power. Stay away from blaming thoughts and take personal responsibility for your problems.

Rev. Don Stewart

There are two things that immediately come to mind when I think of people blaming others for their life problems. One is anger, and the other is being judgmental. The Bible speaks to both of these things. ***"Let all bitterness, and wrath, and anger…be put away from you…And be kind to one another, tenderhearted, forgiving one another…"*** **Ephesians 4:31-32.**

When you feel like someone has done you wrong, God wants your first response to be kindness and forgiveness. I know that will be hard sometimes, but the more you practice kindness and forgiveness, the harder it will be for you to blame that person and have hurtful thoughts about them. (And in turn, your life will be healthier and happier.) In my life there have been plenty of opportunities to put blame on other people and to be angry about it, but the Word of the Lord has always been kindness and forgiveness. ***"Judge not, and you will not be judged: condemn not, and you will not be condemned: forgive, and you will be forgiven."*** **Luke 6:37**

Blame is always followed by judgment. When someone is blamed for a crime, they go to court and if they are guilty, they are judged and sentenced to fines or jail. However, when we blame someone, there is no court for them to plead their case. The person blaming them also automatically judges them. But the sentence of poor health, anxiety, and depression always falls on the person who does the blaming, not the person we accuse of hurting us.

If you want to have healing in your soul, you must practice kindness and forgiveness instead of blaming. When you do this, you will be able to see the situation for what it is and no longer be a victim of your circumstance, but a victor over these thought temptations.

I know a woman – I'll call her Allie. I have known her for 25 years. She is a wonderful lady, but she is so unhappy. In 25 years I've never seen her take responsibility for anything or heard her say one time "I'm sorry," or "I was wrong." She is bitter, unjoyful, and miserable. I've tried to talk to her several times about how she is hurting herself. Although she has been married several times, she still blames her first husband for all her problems. She is very jealous of anyone who gets close to her children and grandchildren. I tried to help her several times, but she continues to play the blame game. One time she seemed to be in a pretty good mood so I started talking to her about forgiveness and I read **Matthew 6:14,15**, ***"For if ye forgive men their trespasses, your heavenly Father will also forgive you; but if ye forgive not men their trespasses, neither will your Father forgive your trespasses. . . ."***

John 20:23, ***"Whose soever sins ye remit, they are remitted unto them; and whose soever sins ye retain, they are retained."***

I explained to her that the word remit means *"to send away"* and the word retain means *"to hold onto."* So the verse literally means whoever's sins you send away from you will be sent away, but whoever's sins you hold onto, they are held there in your heart and you won't be forgiven. So in reality, you take the other person's sin into your heart and you won't be forgiven. You will always play the blame game.

To be forgiven you must send the other person's sin away from you through forgiveness. When you hold onto someone else's sin by not forgiving them, it fractures your personality and causes pain, sickness, and unhappiness. If you don't forgive for anyone else, forgive for yourself and your own welfare. Go forgive others and forgive yourself.

CHAPTER SIXTEEN

The Seven Types Of Depression

Dr. Amen

Depression is not just one thing. Dr. Amen, through his brain imaging work of scanning over 40,000 brains, over the last 15 years, has identified seven different types of depression.

Pure Anxiety

1. Frequent feelings of nervousness or anxiety
2. Panic attacks
3. Avoidance of places for fear of having an anxiety attack
4. Heightened muscle tension (headaches, sore muscles, hand tremors)
5. Periods of heart pounding, nausea, or dizziness
6. Tendency to predict the worst
7. Multiple, persistent fears or phobias (such as dying, doing something crazy)
8. Conflict avoidance
9. Excessive fear of being judged or scrutinized by others
10. Easily startled or tendency to freeze in anxiety-provoking or intense situations.
11. Seemingly shy, timid, and easily embarrassed
12. Bites fingernails or picks skin

Pure Depression

1. Persistent sad or "empty" mood
2. Loss of interest or pleasure in activities that are usually fun, including sex
3. Restlessness, irritability, or excessive crying
4. Feelings of guilt, worthlessness, helplessness, hopelessness, pessimism
5. Sleeping too much or too little, early-morning awakening
6. Appetite and/or weight loss, or overeating and weight gain
7. Decreased energy, fatigue, feeling "slowed down"
8. Thoughts of death or suicide, or suicide attempts
9. Difficulty concentrating, remembering, or making decisions
10. Persistent physical symptoms that do not respond to treatment, such as headaches, digestive disorders, and chronic pain
11. Persistent negativity or chronic low self-esteem
12. Persistent feeling of dissatisfaction or boredom

Mixed Anxiety and Depression

Sufferers of this type have a combination of both Pure Anxiety symptoms and Pure Depression symptoms. This type shows excessive activity in the brain's basal ganglia and the deep limbic system. One type may predominate at any point in time, but both symptom clusters are present on a regular basis.

Over-Focused Anxiety/Depression

Symptoms of Type 4, Over-Focused Anxiety/Depression include at least four items from the Pure Anxiety and/or Pure Depression checklists, plus at least four of the following:

1. Excessive or senseless worrying
2. Upset when things are out of place or don't go the way you planned
3. Tendency to be oppositional or argumentative
4. Tendency to have repetitive negative or anxious thoughts
5. Tendency toward compulsive or addictive behaviors
6. Intense dislike of change
7. Tendency to hold grudges
8. Difficulty seeing options in situations
9. Tendency to hold on to own opinion and not listen to others
10. Need to have things done a certain way or you become very upset
11. Others complain that you worry too much
12. Tend to say no without first thinking about question

Cyclic Anxiety/Depression

The hallmark of this type is a cyclic pattern of anxiety or depression. Symptoms of this type include at least four items from the Pure Anxiety and/or Pure Depression checklists, plus at least four of the following:

1. Periods of abnormally elevated, depressed, or anxious mood
2. Periods of decreased need for sleep, feeling energetic on dramatically less sleep than usual
3. Periods of grandiose notions, ideas, or plans
4. Periods of increased talking or pressured speech
5. Periods of too many thoughts racing through the mind
6. Periods of markedly increased energy
7. Periods of poor judgment that lead to risk-taking behavior (separate from usual behavior)
8. Periods of inappropriate social behavior
9. Periods of irritability or aggression
10. Periods of delusional or psychotic thinking

Temporal Lobe Anxiety/Depression

Symptoms of this type include at least four items from the Pure Anxiety and/or Pure Depression checklists, plus at least four of the following:

1. Short fuse or periods of extreme irritability
2. Periods of rage with little provocation
3. Often misinterprets comments as negative when they are not
4. Periods of spaciness or confusion
5. Periods of panic and/or fear for no specific reason
6. Visual or auditory changes, such as seeing shadows or hearing muffled sounds
7. Frequent periods of déjà vu (feeling of being somewhere you have never been)
8. Sensitivity or mild paranoia
9. Headaches or abdominal pain of uncertain origin
10. History of a head injury or family history of violence or explosiveness
11. Dark thoughts that may involve suicidal or homicidal thoughts
12. Periods of forgetfulness or memory problems

Unfocused Anxiety/Depression

Symptoms of Unfocused Anxiety/Depression include at least four items from the Pure Anxiety and/or Pure Depression checklists, plus at least four of the following:

1. Trouble staying focused
2. Spaciness or feeling in a fog
3. Overwhelmed by tasks of daily living
4. Feeling tired, sluggish, or slow-moving
5. Procrastination, failure to finish things
6. Chronic boredom
7. Loses things
8. Easily distracted
9. Forgetful
10. Poor planning skills
11. Difficulty expressing feelings
12. Difficulty expressing empathy for others

CHAPTER SEVENTEEN
The Six Types Of ADD
Dr. Amen

ADD is not just one thing. Dr. Amen, through his brain imaging work of scanning over 40,000 brains, over the last 15 years, has identified six different types of ADD.

Type 1: Classic ADD

The sufferer:

Is easily distracted

Has difficulty sustaining attention span for most tasks in play, school, or work

Has trouble listening when others are talking

Has difficulty following through (procrastination) on tasks or instructions

Has difficulty keeping an organized area (room, desk, book bag, filing cabinet, locker, etc.)

Has trouble with time, e.g., is frequently late or hurried, tasks take longer than expected, projects or homework are "last-minute" or turned in late

Has a tendency to lose things

Makes careless mistakes, poor attention to detail

Is forgetful

Is restless or hyperactive

Has trouble sitting still

Is fidgety, in constant motion (hands, feet, body)

Is noisy, has a hard time being quiet

Acts as if "driven by a motor"

Talks excessively

Is impulsive (doesn't think through comments or actions before they are said or done)

Has difficulty waiting his or her turn

Interrupts or intrudes on others (e.g., butts into conversations or games)

Type 2: Inattentive ADD

The sufferer:

Is easily distracted

Has difficulty sustaining his or her attention span for most tasks in play, school, or work

Has trouble listening when others are talking

Has difficulty following through (procrastination) on tasks or instructions

Has difficulty keeping an organized area (room, desk, book bag, filing cabinet, locker, etc.)

Has trouble with time, for example, frequently late or hurried, tasks take longer than expected, projects or homework are "last minute" or turned in late

Has a tendency to lose things

Makes careless mistakes, with poor attention to detail

Is forgetful

Daydreams excessively

Complains of being bored

Appears apathetic or unmotivated

Is tired, sluggish, or slow-moving

Is spacy or seems preoccupied

Type 3: Over-Focused ADD

The sufferer has ADD core symptoms, plus:

Worries excessively or senselessly

Is oppositional and argumentative

Has a strong tendency to get locked into negative thoughts, having the same thought over and over

Has a tendency toward compulsive behaviors

Has a tendency to hold grudges

Has trouble shifting attention from subject to subject

Has difficulties seeing options in situations

Has a tendency to hold on to his or her own opinion and not listen to others

Has a tendency to get locked into a course of action, whether or not it is good for him or her

Needs to have things done a certain way or becomes very upset

Is criticized by others for worrying too much

Type 4: Temporal Lobe ADD

The sufferer has ADD core symptoms, plus:

Has periods of quick temper or rages with little provocation

Misinterprets comments as negative when they are not

Has a tendency to become increasingly irritable, then explode, then recede, and is often tired after a rage

Has periods of spaciness or confusion

Has periods of panic and/or fear for no specific reason

Imagines visual changes, such as seeing shadows or objects changing shape

Frequent periods of déjà vu (feelings of being somewhere before even though he or she has never been there)

Is sensitive or mildly paranoid

Experiences headaches or abdominal pain of uncertain origin

Has history of a head injury or family history of violence or explosiveness

Has dark thoughts, may involve suicidal or homicidal ideas

Has periods of forgetfulness or memory problems

Has a short fuse or periods of extreme irritability

Type 5: Limbic ADD

The sufferer has ADD core symptoms, plus:

Moodiness

Negativity

Low energy

Frequent irritability

A tendency to be socially isolated

Frequent feelings of hopelessness, helplessness, or excessive guilt

Lowered interest in things that are usually considered fun

Sleep changes (too much or too little)

Chronic low self-esteem

Type 6: "Ring of Fire" ADD

The sufferer has ADD core symptoms, plus:

Is angry or aggressive

Is sensitive to noise, light, clothes, or touch

Has frequent or cyclic mood changes (highs and lows)

Is inflexible, or rigid in thinking

Insists on having his or her own way, even when told no multiple times

Has periods of mean, nasty, or insensitive behavior

Has periods of excessive talkativeness

Has periods of excessive impulsivity

Exhibits unpredictable behavior

Displays grandiose or "larger than life" thinking

Talks fast

Has the sensation that thoughts go fast

Appears anxious or fearful

CHAPTER EIGHTEEN

Nine Principles To A Healthy Brain

Dr. Amen

1. Your brain is involved with everything you do.

Your brain is involved in every aspect of your life and the person you are. How you think, how you feel, how you act, and how well you get along with other people has to do with the moment-by-moment functioning of your brain. After looking at thousands and thousands of brain scans I have come to realize that how your brain functions influences the kind of person you are, the effectiveness of your mothering skill and how well you do in business.

Are you the kind of person that is on time, listens, and is generally helpful? Likely, your frontal lobes work right. Or, are you the type of person that is often late, interrupts others, and has trouble completing reports in a timely fashion? It may be that you had a frontal lobe injury playing football in high school. Your brain is the command and control center that runs your life.

2. When the brain works right, you work right.

When the brain is troubled, it is hard to be your best self. You generally experience trouble in your relationships, work, or within yourself. Since the brain is well recognized as the organ of behavior, it makes sense that brain problems, such as Alzheimer's disease, attention deficit disorder, schizophrenia or brain trauma is likely to decrease a person's effectiveness in life.

Your success in life is associated with how well your brain works. Will-driven behavior comes from a healthy brain. It allows you to exert conscious choice over a situation to work in your own best interest. Will-driven behavior is goal directed and productive; it helps you reach the goals you have set for your life. As we age, our brains normally get less and less active. A healthy brain, in my experience, is associated with effective, goal-directed behavior. People with healthy brains tend to make the best employers, the best husbands and wives, the best parents, friends, employees, and citizens. People with troubled brains, on the other hand, tend to struggle in all areas of life.

The difference between will-driven and brain-driven behavior: brain-driven behavior occurs when the brain hijacks your will and causes you to act in ways that are unhelpful or even downright destructive. Patients who have obsessive-compulsive disorder (OCD), Touerette's syndrome (TS), or drug abuse are examples of people with potential brain-driven behaviors. A person who suffers from OCD has distressing repetitive thoughts and/or performs compulsive behaviors, such as excessive lock-checking or hand-washing or engaging in elaborate rituals. Even though the person knows these thoughts or behaviors are irrational, he can't just say no to them. They over-think (obsessions) and overact (compulsions).

This principle leads to an important paradigmatic shift: if you see someone who's "not right" then it may not be "them" or their "personality," it may not even be their upbringing or environment (directly) but in the here and now it's a matter of their brain not working properly. WHY it's not working properly is a question not easily answered by saying he or she has a personality disorder, but the "big triumph" comes when people begin to say not "What's the matter with YOU?" but "What's the matter with your BRAIN?" when someone's behaving poorly.

Here's an example of a brain-driven behavior. People with attention deficit disorder (ADD) are often chronically late and disorganized. Many imaging studies report that ADD is associated with low prefrontal cortex activity, the part of the brain responsible for forethought, judgment, impulse control, and organization. When your brain works right, you work right. When your brain is troubled, it is very hard for you to be your best self. There is much hope, but it is critical to start with the information that your brain matters and that taking care of it needs to be part of your life.

3. The brain is the most complicated organ in the universe. There is nothing as complex as the human brain. Nothing. Your brain is the most complex, mind-blowing organ in the universe! It weighs only about three pounds, usually around 2 percent of the body's weight. Unbelievably, given that it is the bedrock of the personality – some think even the soul – it is 80 percent water!

The brain contains more than a hundred billion neurons (also called nerve cells or brain cells), which is about the number of stars in the Milky Way Galaxy. It is estimated that we have 100 billion neurons or nerve cells and trillions of supportive brain cells called glial cells. Each neuron is connected to other neurons by up to 40,000 individual connections between cells. You have more connections in your brain than there are stars in the universe. Also, even though your brain is only about two percent of your body's weight, it uses twenty five to thirty percent of the calories you consume. Your brain is the major energy consumer in the body.

It's commonly said that we only use 10 percent of our brains. Nonsense! You may not use every neuron in your brain at the same time, but each one is important. The brain never turns off or even rests throughout your entire life. It is very active at night, especially during dreaming. In order to work properly, the brain needs fuel, oxygen, and stimulation. Just like any other living thing, a brain needs fuel to grow, function, and repair itself. Glucose and oxygen run the engine powered by the brain cells.

The brain needs oxygen to produce energy; without it, the energy powerhouses of neurons called mitochondria would not produce enough energy to keep your brain alive. Because blood delivers glucose and oxygen to the brain, nothing must get in the way of blood flow if the brain is to stay healthy. The best sources of stimulation for the brain are physical exercise, mental exercise, and social bonding. If, as the New Testament says, the body is the temple of the Holy Spirit, certainly the brain is the inner sanctum.

4. Your brain is very soft, yet it is housed in a very hard skull that has many ridges. Mild traumatic brain injuries can change people's whole lives and virtually no one knows it, because mental health professionals never look at brain function. Understanding this point means that we should not let children hit soccer balls with their heads; tackle football is really a form of child abuse; and as professionals, we need to take even mild traumatic brain injuries seriously. Clinically, I have found that I have to ask patients at least 5 times whether or not they have had a serious brain injury. Often they forget, and therapists give them the diagnoses of personality disorders, when, in fact, they have brain damage from injuries or accidents.

When the brain is alive, and pulsating with activity, it is like a delicate, intricate, organized spider-web suspended in crystal-clear fluid. The consistency of the brain has been described as being similar to soft butter, custard, and tofu or somewhere between egg whites and Jell-O. It is 85 percent water. Yet we often think of the brain as a firm, rubbery substance, mostly because the brains dissected in anatomy labs and the ones shown on TV were fixed in formaldehyde.

One of the most important lessons I've learned from looking at more than forty thousand brain scans is that brain injuries, even "mild" ones without a loss of consciousness, matter more than most people, including doctors, think. Millions of people in our society have suffered significant brain injuries, yet no one knows about it.

Your brain lives in a closed space. When you experience a blow to the head, there is no place for the brain to go, so it ends up slamming against the walls, ridges, and sharp body edges in the skull, ripping small blood vessels, causing multiple minute bleeds and, over time, many areas of tiny scars. Brain injuries tend to be additive. When an injury damages a certain part of the brain, not all people have symptoms, because the brain has built-in reserves. A concussion or mild "traumatic brain injury" (TBI) is far more than just a bump on the head. According to the American Academy of Neurology, "There is no such thing as a minor concussion." A study from UCLA found that "the level of brain glucose use in people who suffered mild concussions was similar to that in comatose, severely brain-injured patients. ...Even mild head injuries result in major changes to the brain's metabolism and could make victims susceptible to more serious damage from a repeated blow." While often there are no immediate symptoms with a concussion and nothing irregular shows up on the CT scan or the MRI, subtle changes occur.

Over a period of a few weeks or even months, the individual may become tearful, angry, or irritable; have trouble thinking clearly or concentrating; or suffer from headaches, confusion, blurred vision, memory loss, or nausea. Other devastating symptoms can occur as if in slow motion. There may be personality changes, temper problems, dark thoughts, and difficulty expressing emotions or understanding others.

Brain injuries can interrupt, delay, or alter social and intellectual development, sometimes seriously. Think about your brain before you do activities that might put it at risk. Kids must wear protective gear while playing football and hockey; do not let them hit soccer balls with their heads, and encourage them to play non-contact sports. Always wear a helmet when you ride a bike (even as an adult). Walk facing automobile traffic, not with your back toward it. Never shake a baby or toddler.

The good news is that brain injuries can be treated. Medication, therapy, and cognitive retraining have all been found to be helpful. We cannot prevent all injuries, so early diagnosis and proper treatment is essential. The most important strategy for us as a society is to prevent injuries by respecting the brain and stopping reckless, stupid behavior. Your brain matters. Respect and protect it!

5. **Certain parts of the brain tend to do certain things.** For example, the prefrontal cortex is involved with executive functions; the temporal lobes are involved with memory, auditory processing, word finding and emotional reactions; the parietal lobes are involved with direction sense; etc. Understanding psychobiology is critical to taking a new view of psychiatric illness.

6. **Problems in certain brain areas are often associated with specific learning, behavioral or emotional problems.** If there are prefrontal cortex issues one would expect there to be executive function problems, such as short attention span, disorganization, poor planning and impulse control issues. If there are temporal lobe problems it is likely people will exhibit struggles with memory, mood stability, word finding and temper control. If there are parietal lobe issues people may get lost

easily. Knowing about brain pathology will allow clinicians to target treatments to brain areas rather than just nebulous psychiatric diagnoses. With this model, clinicians develop prefrontal cortex treatments, temporal lobe treatments, etc.

Most problems (such as ADD, anxiety, and depression) are not single or simple disorders. One size does not fit everyone; people need an individualized approach to optimizing their brain and their life. If you treat all patients with the same group of symptoms the same way, you will make some people better and a lot of people worse. In our experience, attention deficit disorder is not one illness but rather at least six different sets of problems, and if doctors immediately turn to stimulant medications for everyone who has ADD, they make four of the six types worse. Anxiety and depression are not separate homogeneous problems, but rather a combination of overlapping issues with at least seven different subtypes. While Prozac-like medications may work perfectly for some, giving all people with depression the same type of drug invites treatment failures and in some cases may cause suicide or homicide attempts.

Each person needs an individualized treatment plan based on the problems in his or her own specific brain. Doctors should be treating not symptoms, but rather the underlying brain problems that are causing the difficulties.

The Amen Clinics use a brain system approach for diagnosing and treating problems. We believe that problems such as ADD, anxiety, and depression are overall categories and that effective treatment takes into account individual variations within each type. In addition, we know that there are many ways, in addition to medicine, to help balance the brain. It is our job to inform people about what they have and give them different treatment options so they can decide what is best for them.

One treatment does not fit everyone. We are all different and have different needs. Individualizing interventions for you and for your specific brain is important to making a good brain great!

7. Most psychiatric illnesses are not single or simple disorders. Giving someone the diagnosis of major depression is akin to giving patients the diagnosis of chest pain. Why don't we give people the diagnosis of chest pain? Because chest pain is a symptom with many potential causes, such as heart or lung disease, musculoskeletal problems, abdominal or back problems, as well as grief or panic attacks.

Unfortunately, in psychiatry we give people simple diagnoses, such as major depression, ADD, or bipolar disorder, that represent symptom clusters without understanding the richness of the potential underlying causes. This leads to overly simplistic treatments that make some better and many worse. Our brain imaging work has classified 6 different types of ADD and 7 different types of anxiety and depression. Understanding the types helps us be better at targeting treatments to specific brain areas. We use imaging technology to help us make difficult brains better and good brains great, because it allows us to obtain a baseline to evaluate brain health. Like whole-body scans, brain imaging is now at the point where we can specifically see how the brain works and make targeted interventions to help it.

We can see who needs help and who doesn't. Imaging allows us to see if your brain is working too hard in certain areas or not hard enough. It allows us to visualize if your brain has been hurt, traumatized, or exposed to toxic chemicals. It allows us to give people targeted help and then do follow-up scans to see if we are making the progress we want.

Imaging the brain is essential to knowing how to help it. Imaging helps physicians be more effective, increases patients' compliance, and decreases stigma. Imaging helps give direction on how to make a good brain great!

The lack of brain imaging, in my opinion, has kept psychiatry lagging behind medicine's other specialties, decreasing its effectiveness with patients, and reinforcing the stigma that surrounds people who struggle with mood, or learning behavior problems. It is time to work toward using imaging on a daily basis to look at people who struggle, and also at people who want to be better than they are. I am trained as a psychiatrist with psychoanalytic roots. I also have a specialty in children, teenagers, families, and brain imaging. There are so many different causes of behavior, learning, and emotional problems that I think it is unconscionable for physicians not to look at the brain, the organ of behavior, learning, and emotion.

The brain is the organ of behavior, and imaging technology can be helpful and vital to people today. At the Amen Clinics, because of our experience, we have added these further reasons to get a scan: to evaluate violence, suicidal behavior, substance abuse, sub-typing ADD, anxiety and depression, and complex or resistant psychiatric problems, and to evaluate brain health for determining appropriate prevention strategies.

8. Imaging the brain helps mental health professionals be more effective, decreases stigma and increases compliance for patients. Imaging the brain also teaches mental health professionals to ask more informed questions. Why are psychiatrists (and I would argue psychologists) the only medical professionals that never look at the organ they treat? You can try to kill yourself today in Los Angeles and virtually no one outside of our clinics will look at the patient's brain. Cardiologists, orthopedists, gynecologists, gastroenterologists, and ophthalmologists all look at what they do before they do it. It would be considered malpractice in almost all areas of medicine to treat patients solely based on history.

Yet, isn't that what we do in mental health? We have had great tools to look at brain function for more than a decade. So why don't we look? Several reasons: imaging the brain is not part of our training, experience or tradition. UC, Irvine is the only psychiatric residency program that teaches residents how to use imaging tools clinically. It is time to change. The brain is our organ and we need more information to do the best job for our clients and stop guessing what might be the problem.

The study we do in our clinic is called brain **SPECT** imaging. **SPECT** stands for **single photon emission computed tomography** and measures blood flow and activity patterns in the brain. It basically tells us three things: areas of the brain that work well, areas of the brain that work too hard and areas of the brain that do not work hard enough. Once we know how the brain works, the goal of treatment is to balance brain function, such as calm the overactive areas and enhance the under active ones.

9. THE BRAIN CAN CHANGE. You can change your brain and change your life! This is the headline for mental health in the new millennium! When we do the right things for our clients, whether it is great psychotherapy, effective use of medication or supplements, or newer treatments such as transcranial magnetic stimulation or hyperbaric oxygen treatment we enhance brain function and enhance people's lives. My best-selling book, *"Change Your Brain, Change Your Life"* is centered on this principle. We have seen it work for more than 15 years. The brain is adaptive and influenced by what we do for it.

The opposite is also true; the brain can change in a negative way when we do the wrong things. Yes, you can impair brain function with the wrong interventions. We must have great respect for our interventions. I argue that we need to look at the brain before we do things to it and also check ourselves periodically to see if we are making things better or worse.

Very few people have perfect brains. We all need a little help! When I first started my brain-imaging work, I was not very concerned with the concept of normal, because I had so many sick people to try to help. In our client database, we have more than sixty murderers and hundreds of violent people. We have thousands of patients with ADD, anxiety, depression, brain trauma, substance abuse, and bipolar disorder. But building a database of normal people also became essential to my work. We needed normal people to do comparison studies on our patient group and to be able to understand and publish our results.

I knew that finding normal people would be a challenge. The people who I thought were normal often ended up in my office asking for help. Still, I had no idea how hard it would be to find truly normal brains. The research team was amazed that so many people who thought of themselves as not only normal but almost perfect were in reality troubled with mood or attention problems or had histories of serious brain injury or forgotten substance abuse.

We now believe that normal is a myth and healthy brains are actually rare. There are very few healthy brains among us. We all need a little help. It helps us see that brain health is fragile and must be taken seriously. And as a society, we need to make brain health a priority.

We have found that many people who struggle do not know that they have problems. Did you know that 95 percent of people who have Alzheimer's disease are not diagnosed until they are in the moderate-to-severe stages of the illness? Clearly, it is much better to know that a problem is brewing early, so you can implement prevention and treatment strategies as soon as possible. Many people do not know that they have sustained brain injuries that have affected their lives. Many people also have no idea that they have mood or attention problems; yet ask their spouses, and you will get an earful.

If we all need a little help, then early screening is an essential tool for keeping our brains healthy as we age!

Chapter Nineteen

Healing The Soul

Rev. Don Stewart

What do you think of when you hear this name: *Mother Teresa*? You probably think of someone who was totally dedicated to helping the poor and destitute; someone who was close to God. You might even call her a saint. It's quite obvious to me that she suffered from depression. The September 3, 2007, edition of *Time* Magazine reveals some of the letters she wrote. She doubted her faith. She wrote:

> *"Lord, my God, who am I that You should forsake me? The Child of Your Love – and now, become as the most hated one – the one – You have thrown away as unwanted – unloved. I call, I cling, I want – and there is no One to answer – no One on Whom I can cling – no, No One. – Alone... Where is my Faith – even deep down right in there is nothing, but emptiness & darkness – My God – how powerful is this unknown pain – I have no Faith – I dare not utter the words & thoughts that crowd in my heart – & make me suffer untold agony. So many unanswered questions live within me afraid to uncover them – because of the blasphemy – If there be God – please forgive me – When I try to raise my thoughts to Heaven – there is such convicting emptiness that those very thoughts return like sharp knives and hurt my very soul. – I am told God loves me – and yet the reality of darkness & coldness & emptiness is so great that nothing touches*

my soul. Did I make a mistake in surrendering blindly to the Call of the Sacred Heart?"

Here is a woman who totally dedicated her life to helping the poor and destitute, respected around the world. She prayed every morning at 4:30 a.m., yet she doubted her faith, had feelings of emptiness, despair and pain.

I ask myself the questions: did this suffering take place because of her Roman Catholic theology? Did she identify so much with the poor and destitute that she took on their suffering? Could she have been helped? Did she want to be helped? Where could she have gone to receive help? Did she have a brain problem? Whatever the case was it's obvious to me that she didn't suffer because she wasn't strong or had weak character. So don't beat yourself up or allow anyone else to put guilt on you because you are dealing with anxiety or depression.

Jack came to my meeting in Cincinnati, Ohio sometime ago. He had suffered from depression for years. He self medicated with alcohol and drugs. He came forward, accepted Christ as his Savior and was filled with the Holy Ghost. I worked with him about his attitude, his negative thinking and speaking. I told him to start confessing who he is in Christ and what the Word of God says he is. We developed an affirmation for him to say every time a negative thought came into his mind or he felt tempted to use alcohol or drugs.

I am who God says I am.

I can do all things in Christ.

I am more than a conqueror.

I am renewed in the spirit of my mind.

I have the mind of Christ.

My soul prospers and I walk in health and prosperity.

I fear no evil.

I am the righteousness of God in Christ Jesus. Amen.

Jack put this on a card and carried it with him everywhere he went, pulling it out of his pocket many times a day until he memorized it. In fact, he carried it with him for several years just to remind him – he was delivered from his alcohol and drugs. I don't mean to imply he never had any more temptations or trials, but he was stable, happy and filled with joy, able to live a very productive life.

He told me that he still battled with depression. I suggested he may want to see a doctor, also that some cognitive therapy might help him. He went on an antidepressant for a while; it helped. He eventually was able to get off the medicine, and with therapy to help him with his thoughts, he has been able to live a very productive, successful life. He told me that he felt that he needed the medicine and therapy to help him, but the affirmation about who he was in God was the most helpful. A good description of what depression feels like is found in the Bible. **Deuteronomy 28:67: *"In the morning thou shalt say, Would God it were even! and at even thou shalt say, Would God it were morning! for the fear of thine heart wherewith thou shalt fear, and for the sight of thine eyes which thou shalt see."***

In our society, and in some church circles, depression is looked upon as some kind of character weakness – sin in your life – failure on your part. But this is not always the case. If you have to wear glasses to help you see, does that mean there is sin in your life? Sometimes the brain, the hardware of your soul, needs to be healed.

There is HOPE for you!

There is help for you through

HEALING THE SOUL AND BRAIN!

Here are a couple of Steps for you to take Right Now.

STEP 1: **Receive Forgiveness – Give Forgiveness**

Jesus said, ***"If you don't forgive, you shall not be forgiven."*** **Matthew 6:15**

Accept Christ as your Savior. Become born again. Ask Christ to come into your life.

"Old things are passed away; behold, all things are become new." **2 Corinthians 5:17**

STEP 2: **Have the mind of Christ. *"Be renewed in the spirit of your mind."* Ephesians 4:23**

David said, ***"He restored my soul"*** **Psalm 23:3**

"As a man thinketh in his heart, so is he." **Proverbs 23:7**

Please pray this prayer with me:

"Dear Lord, please come into my heart and forgive me of my sins. I now accept You over my life. Please heal my soul and let Your peace live in me." Amen

Normal Healthy Brain

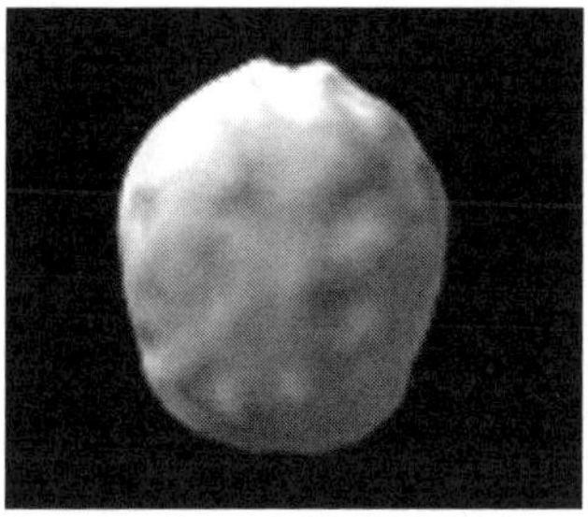

An overhead SPECT scan of a normal healthy brain.

Depressed Brain Underside View

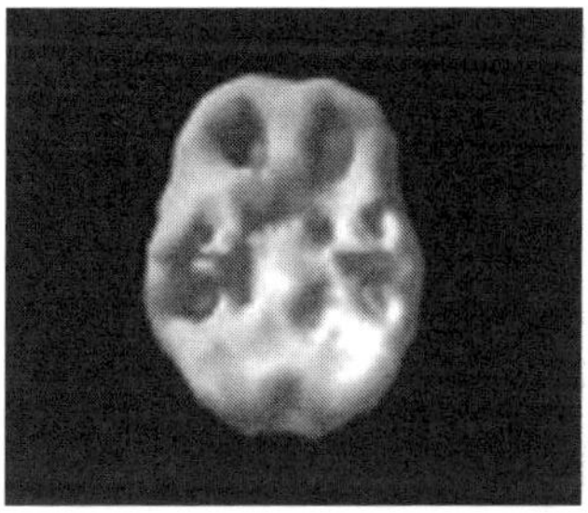

The brain of a 17 year old girl with depression and suicidal thoughts

ADD Brain Under Concentration

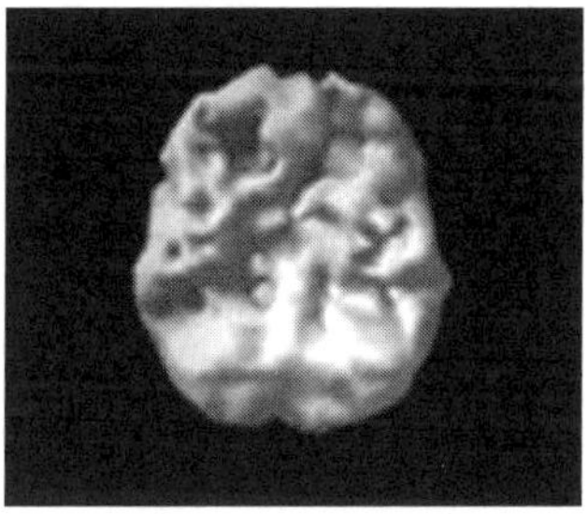

Brain with the AD/HD subtype of ADD while under concentration

Top Down Surface View of Alcoholic's Brain

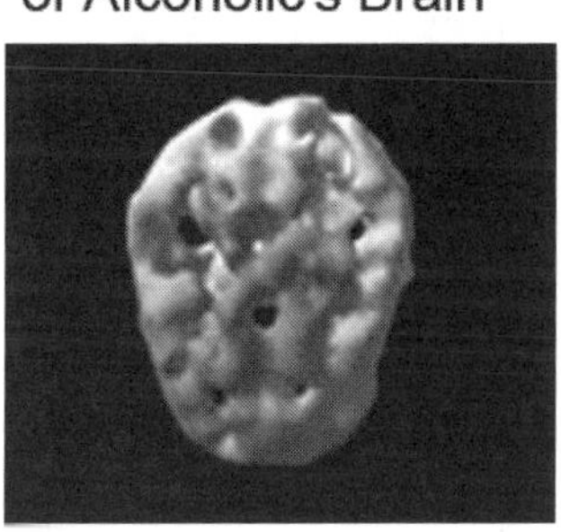

The brain of a 38 year old with 17 years of heavy weekend drinking.

Paranoid Schizophrenic Brain

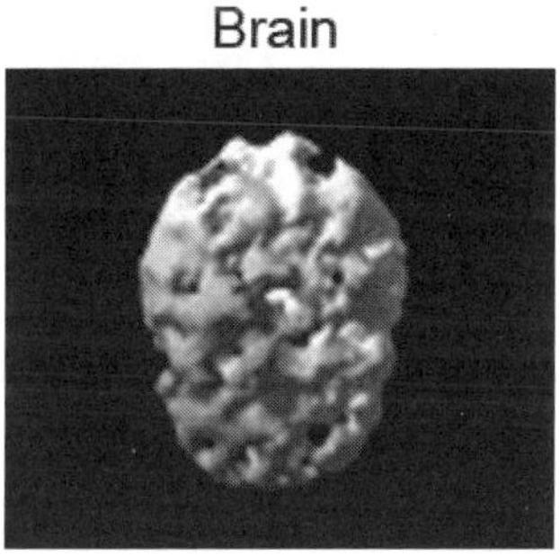

Brain with marked decrease of activity throughout the celebral cortex.

A.A. Allen, my spiritual father and mentor.

1950's Aerial shot of A.A. Allen's Crusade tent.

A.A. Allen and me, preaching under the big Gospel tent.

People loved seeing miracles as they occurred.

Inside the tent in the 1950s

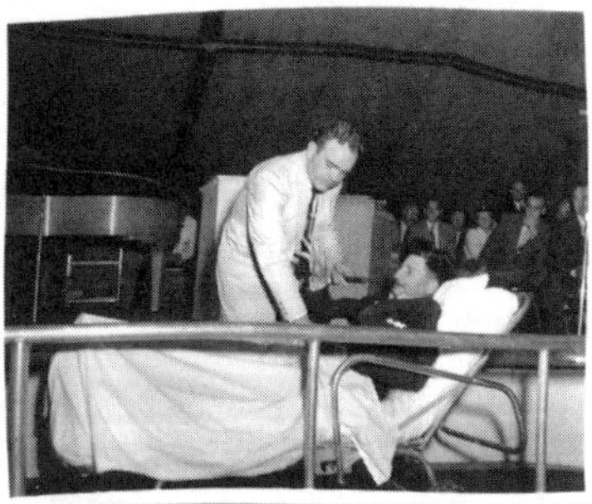

Prayer lines often included people on stretchers...and many were healed.

Me in 1965, speaking in Phoenix, Arizona

Signs, Wonders and Miracles. In my crusades I have been blessed to see the lame walk, the deaf hear, and the blind see...

An African man and I sharing in one of the many Miracles I have been blessed to be a part of.

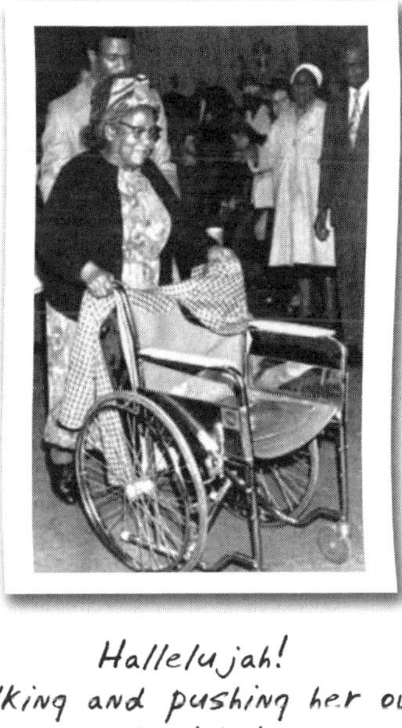

Hallelujah!
Walking and pushing her own wheelchair.

1980 Crusade in
El Salvador

A crusade at Araneta
Coliseum in the 1970's. At
that time, Araneta was
the largest coliseum in
the world.

One of my favorite shots
1978 Brazil
South America

I was told I was the 1st healing
evangelist to ever fill Madison
Square Garden

Countless people in over 80 countries around the world have come forward to commit their lives to Jesus!

Let's give God all the glory!

Over half a million people attended the service in Nigeria when God miraculously healed this young woman and many others.

Hallelujah! She doesn't need her walker anymore!

"Be healed in Jesus' mighty name!"

2007 Me, Don Stewart, on the set of my "Power and Mercy" TV program.